Taking a Look Back
in Order to Move Forward

TAKING a LOOK BACK in ORDER to MOVE FORWARD

Tina M. Sharp

XULON PRESS

Xulon Press
2301 Lucien Way #415
Maitland, FL 32751
407.339.4217
www.xulonpress.com

© 2019 by Tina M. Sharp

All rights reserved solely by the author. The author guarantees all contents are original and do not infringe upon the legal rights of any other person or work. No part of this book may be reproduced in any form without the permission of the author. The views expressed in this book are not necessarily those of the publisher.

Unless otherwise indicated, Scripture quotations taken from the King James Version (KJV)–*public domain*.

Printed in the United States of America.

ISBN-13: 978-1-5456-7216-7

Dedication

Above all else, I would like to dedicate this book to my heavenly Father and my Lord and Savior Jesus Christ. Also, to my loving mother who fought the good fight of faith during her battle with cancer, in loving memory of Stella Mae Berry. I want to dedicate this book also to my husband who's been there through it all. I'm grateful and thankful he was able to push himself at a young age to go after his dreams. I'm grateful for him taking care of me and our family. I'm thankful for the man he has become. I'm thankful for him being a loving husband and awesome dad.

To my two wonderful daughters, I'm very proud of who you've become. I'm proud of the way you support each other in your life's endeavors. Thank you for supporting me all the way through writing this book. Thank you for your unwavering support. I don't think I could have done it without you. I'm truly blessed to have you as daughters. I love you both.

Acknowledgments

I would like to acknowledge my entire family: my husband Johnny Sharp, my two daughters Renishia Sharp and Tenishia Sharp, and my pastors Kelvin and Ginger Morgan. I would like to thank all of my sponsors who donated toward publishing this book. There are too many to name individually. Thank you from the bottom of my heart. You all know who you are. I want to also acknowledge my longtime friends Sheila Peterson, Detra Cook, and Phoebe Johnson for giving me the belief this endeavor was possible and could be accomplished if I believed in myself. Thank you, everybody who supported me along the way. Thanks so much.

Introduction

This book will explain the importance of taking a look back in order to move forward in your life. It will help you to put your life in perspective. Upon completing this book, you will gain a greater understanding of your life's journey, and that understanding will allow you to let go of the things in the past and help you move forward. You will start to understand how all the things you have gone through in life have shaped and molded you into the person you are today. Sometimes we forget all the ups and downs we have gone through. But the good thing about it is, you're still here, and you're still standing.

Please note as you read this book that it is not written in sequential order, but it is based upon various life memories.

Contents

1. How It All Began........................1
   The Judge
   Renewed Wedding Vows

2. The Early Years: School after School..........7
   The First Time We Met

3. Surprise, Surprise 11
   The Saddest Day
   The Biggest Mistake
   Encounter with God
   Back to the Story

4. Leaving Riverside Behind.................21
   Dad's Confession

5. Losing Mom 29
   Adversaries

6. Mom's Funeral 37
   Missing You
   I Had a Dream

7. Family Letters 43
   Daughter's Father's Day Card

8. Finger Injury........................... 49

9. The Dog 53

10. When You Don't Listen to Your Mother 59
    Coming Home
    Back Down Memory Lane
    The Fighting Siblings

11. Commodity Food 67
    Thanksgiving and Christmas
    Moving on Up
    Family Reunion

12. Reno, Pink Glass, Not Even Crystal
    Flamingos 73
    Vegas, Baby! Here We Come!

13. The Stolen Car 77
    The Night the Television Got Stolen

14. Motherhood. 81
    Section 8
    Home Sweet Home
    Forgetting the Past

15. Never Too Much 89

16. The Love of Basketball .93
    Reminiscing
    Life-Changing Decision

17. Fresno, Here We Come 99
    Hawaiian Sand

18. Finally Letting Go. 105

19. Taking a Look Back in Order to
    Move Forward. 111

Chapter 1
How It All Began

One day my husband came home from work and asked me for our marriage license so he could renew the medical insurance policy for his job. He said he needed to show proof we were married so I could be added to the policy. When he asked me for the license, I thought to myself, "Where is our marriage license?" I looked everywhere and couldn't find it.

Eventually my husband said he would call the Hall of Records in San Bernardino, California, where we were married, and request a copy. When he called the Hall of Records, they told him there would be a twelve-dollar fee for them to search and send a copy of the marriage license to him. So, he paid the fee. About a week went by, and I checked the mail daily, until finally, a big yellow envelope arrived.

My spouse opened the envelope and pulled out a white certificate. As he began to read the certificate, he started to look a little strange. I asked him, "What's the matter?"

He said, "The letter stated there was no marriage license located on file." As we both sat there in amazement and thought about the letter we had just received, we came to the realization that neither one of us had ever remembered seeing our marriage license. The next day, we went down to the records department in Fresno, California, where we currently lived. I explained to the clerk that the letter we received in the mail was based on a search conducted by the Hall of Records Department in San Bernardino, California, which did a comprehensive search in both counties—San Bernardino as well as Los Angeles—to see if they could locate our marriage certificate. They were unsuccessful in finding our marriage license in either county.

By this time, I was starting to get a little nervous; our marriage license wasn't showing up. We were seventeen and eighteen, respectively, when we were married, and here it was thirty-five years later. It was a little strange no one could locate the marriage license. The receptionist at the Hall of Records told us if we could prove we were in fact married, and a ceremony did take place, then we were going to have to go to court and do an amendment. The purpose of the amendment was to have our license issued to us without having to get remarried and lose all of our history as a married couple.

When you've been married for years, you start to accumulate possessions. If there ever was a situation where you had to divorce, no one would be entitled to any of the possessions. You would have to split them up. Even if you had a prenuptial, it would not stand up in a court of law. You would have to divide those possessions gained through the years. So, we went home with all the necessary paperwork to fill out and had all the information we needed in order to gather up all our documentation. We had step-by-step instructions on what we needed to do so we could get this matter resolved. I got all our wedding pictures and notarized letters from friends and family who attended our wedding celebration. So, we went to the courthouse to pay the fees and set a date to see the judge. I hoped with the proof I had obtained, it would be enough for the judge to acknowledge we were indeed married.

The Judge

Finally, the day came for us to go before a judge to prove our marriage was valid. We provided all the requested documents to the judge to access while we explained our situation of not being able to locate our certificate of marriage. The judge quickly reviewed the information and then stated to us we should seek representation from a lawyer to deal with this matter. When I contacted a lawyer, their firm explained to me, I would be charged another fee for them to do research. The research the lawyer's firm acknowledged they would be performing wasn't much more than what I had already done. We decided not to use the lawyer's firm and to pursue it ourselves. We went back to court a month later, and the judge scheduled a continuance. The third time we went to court, the judge then denied our claim and told us the best thing for us to do was to get married again.

We were both shocked and devastated, at the same time, from the information we had just received. I was starting to get stressed out from the idea that, if we were to marry again, all the thirty-five years we had already put into the marriage would be voided. Neither of us could do anything to fix our situation, and the thought that we were not actually legally married after thirty-five years was devastating. I was seventeen and my husband-to-be was eighteen when we first took our vows. My mother had to give permission for me to be married at the time because I was a minor, and as a minor, your parents or guardian had to sign documents, stating they gave their permission for you to marry, in order to make your marriage legal. The pastor who counseled and married us was my mother's cousin. He never asked us if we had a marriage certificate to sign at any time, during or after the wedding.

Renewed Wedding Vows

Now, here's where it starts to get interesting. My husband and I had renewed our wedding vows on at least three different occasions. After fifteen years of marriage, we went to Las Vegas to renew our vows for our fifteenth anniversary. At the time, we had no idea there was no marriage certificate on file. The second time we renewed our vows was in Fresno, where we presently live. We renewed them at our church when our pastors decided to have all married couples renew their commitments to each other during an overnight shut-in. The third time we renewed our vows was at the church, once again, during a Valentine ceremony. Mind you, all of this was taking place with us being unaware of our current situation, which was that we did not have a marriage certificate on record.

Once we found out there was no certificate on file, the judge told us she could not do anything about it. We did the only thing we could do; we decided to get remarried. We thought we were married once, and we thought we renewed our wedding vows three other times. Finally, we had to—quote, unquote—really get married, for what constituted our first time. All in all, we went through this ritual four times before we finally got it right, but only one counted. Never would I have thought I would be going through something like this almost thirty-five years later.

Chapter 2
The Early Years: School after School

When I first went to junior high school, I remember our physical education (PE) teacher telling us we had to take a mandatory shower after our PE class. I was in shock because I was so shy. To take off my clothes in front of other girls was something I was not used to doing. I didn't know how to feel. I was just starting to develop breasts. So, I devised a plan to get into the locker room first before anyone else. I would hurry up and take my shower and get dressed before the other girls came in. My mom told me being shy was normal. It took me a little while to get over being shy and undressing and showering in front of others. I thought to myself, first of all, everyone had to shower. We were all the same age, and it was new to everyone. So, I thought, the other girls were probably experiencing the same emotions as I was. I eventually got over it after a few weeks, and the rest of the year went by pretty fast after that.

After graduating from junior high school, my brother and I went to Montclair High School, in Montclair California. Montclair High School was not in our school district, and our mom had to use someone else's address in order for us to attend this school. We wanted to go to Montclair High School because all of our friends went to Montclair High. My brother and I knew we could not get into any trouble, because of the address we were using. Mom always told us, "Do not draw any attention to yourselves." Right from the beginning, my brother would go to school, but he wouldn't go to class. I would see him ditching class. Although we were warned not to get into any trouble and bring awareness to our situation, my brother was always getting into fights.

One day after school, a boy punched my brother in the mouth and split his lip wide open. I can remember blood being all over his shirt. The next day, he got in a fight with the wrestling coach. He was sent to the office. They called me over the school speaker, asking me to go to the office. Because of all the trouble my brother kept getting into, we eventually had to go to another school because they found out we were not in the Montclair School District.

The First Time We Met

Because of the district we lived in, we had to go to a school called Pomona High School. I didn't want to go to Pomona High School because I heard it was a predominately black school. I was nervous about going there, but we did eventually enroll. This is where I met my boyfriend and eventual husband. I had only been at Pomona High for a couple of days when I saw this guy with a big, round head of hair, called a natural, coming toward me. He stopped me and asked me my name. I was so shy, I started laughing and told him my name.

He asked me if I was a new student there. I started laughing again and said, "Yes, I came from Montclair High School." He said he hoped to see me again and started walking away. After taking several steps, he turned and looked back. I also turned and looked back.

The next day I saw him again, this time in the indoor hallway. Now mind you, I didn't even have a class in the indoor hallway. I wanted to make sure I saw him again. I figured if I had seen him over there the day before, I might get lucky and see him again. Sure enough, there he was. This time he asked me for my phone number. I laughed and said, "I do not have any paper." So, he asked his friend, whom he was walking with, to give him some paper. His friend gave him a whole sheet of paper. He said, "I hope this is big enough for you to write your number on." I started laughing again and wrote my number down. He said he would call me. Once again, he started walking away and after a few steps turned around and looked back at me. I did the same. After a few days, he finally called me. On the first call, we talked for hours. This became a regular routine for both of us. We would talk on the phone, some nights until three o'clock in the morning. It got to a point to where we would fall asleep on the phone.

We officially started dating after a couple of weeks. I stopped going to some of my classes because I would leave campus to go home with him. Mainly, all we did was kiss and touch. We were together just about six months before he wanted to start having sex. I was really nervous because I was a virgin and didn't know if I was ready. He was my first real boyfriend, so when he started to pressure me into having sex with him, I didn't know how to handle it; but I really liked him, so

I decided to go through with it. I knew he was the one I wanted to be with.

I eventually told this story to my daughters of how their dad and I met. I told them how he came over to my house one night and how I hid him in the closet with no clothes on. My room was right next to the bathroom. All of a sudden, we heard one of my family members walking by my room. I was so scared my mom was going to come in the room and catch us. But the next day, my brother told me it was he who was walking by my bedroom door. He told me he heard us in the room, but he never told on me.

Chapter 3
Surprise, Surprise

Two months later, I started feeling sick, and my mother took me to our family doctor. The doctor checked me out and ran some tests and wanted my mother to take the bloodwork to another lab where it could be tested. I remember going home and sleeping most of the day. My mother left me home with my older brother and sister as she ran errands. While we were at home, the phone rang. My sister ran to answer the phone and said it was the doctor's office calling. My sister couldn't wait to tell my mom the doctor had called.

When Mom got home, my sister told her, "The doctor called!" My mother went right away and called the doctor back. The doctor told my mother I was pregnant. When my mother got off the phone, she came right into my room and confronted me about being pregnant. I sat up and looked at her in shock and said, "No, I can't be."

I remember the look on her face. She was hurt and disappointed. She said she knew that boy wasn't riding his bike over here in the rain for nothing. My mother talked to me about being too young to be having a baby. That's when I knew I had let her down. We talked about me having an abortion. I wasn't sure what to think, but I said okay.

Saddest Day

I remember going to the hospital. We checked in early in the morning. I was really scared. I was in my room waiting for the procedure to take place, my mother having left me there all alone, not knowing how long of a wait it would be. As soon as she left, the nurses came in to get me. I had no time to call Mom to let her know the doctor was about to perform the operation. I was all alone and scared. I had all these doctors around me, preparing me for this gut-wrenching procedure.

I recall going to sleep and waking up in my room, thinking it was all over. About an hour later, the doctor came in and explained to me they were unable to do the abortion because I was too far along. I couldn't believe what I was hearing. The doctor went on to tell me there was still another procedure that could be done, but I would have to go to a different facility. This procedure would involve the doctor putting me into labor, and he wanted me to think about it.

I called my mother and explained to her everything the doctor had told me. Right away, my mother said, "No, I'm coming to get you, and you're going to have this baby." I felt kind of relieved and happy at the same time. Later, my mother told me she had been praying about it at church. I called my boyfriend and told him what had happened, thinking he would be mad at me for not having the abortion. He was surprised about it and really felt he was too young to be a dad. I felt the same way about being a mother. Eventually, he admitted he was happy we would be keeping the baby. I admitted I was also happy I was keeping the baby.

Surprise, Surprise

I immediately left school and checked into a continuation school. See, times were different then. Nowadays, when students get pregnant, they just stay in school and finish right there at the same school. Schools are now set up for such an occasion. In fact, a young teen can have a child and still continue her education. She can have her baby at the same school while she is in school. She can go visit and feed her child during school. In fact, they have child-care classes for the mother to help teach her how to take care of her child.

Back when I was in school, it wasn't openly accepted to stay in school when you got pregnant. So, if someone was at school one week and gone the next, it was assumed she got pregnant. I left, not because of the shame of being pregnant, but because I didn't want to be judged by my friends. People were so judgmental. So, I didn't graduate from Pomona High School. I graduated from Park West Continuation School. It was disappointing that I didn't get a chance to graduate with my class or go to prom with my classmates. There was one benefit of graduating from Park West Continuation School. I got the chance to graduate early. Although I walked across the stage pregnant and was as big as a house, mind you, I was thankful to be finally finished with school and that chapter of my life.

After I had my baby, I moved out of my mother's home and into an apartment and called my boyfriend to move in with me. At first his mother was hesitant and didn't want us living together, but he did anyway. Both parents thought we were too young to be living together, but we were a family now and had to grow up quickly. I had been saving money from being on Aid to Families with Dependent Children (AFDC), which was just a fancy way of saying welfare. That's how I was able to move. Although my boyfriend moved in with me, he had to get a job.

We didn't have a car at the time, so he would ride his bike to work. We lived in a one-bedroom apartment with a six-month-old baby. The bike that my boyfriend rode to work every day was an old ten-speed bike. The bike was in such bad shape that it didn't have any brake controls. In order to stop the bike, he had to tie a piece of rope from the back of his seat to the brake control. Whenever he wanted to stop or slow down, he had to reach behind him and pull on the rope, tied to his seat and the brake control. He mentioned there were times when he spilled out because of the algae that was in the water drains. This was his only means of transportation until we were able to finally get a car.

My mother would call me every day to check on her granddaughter and see how she was doing. My mom and I would also talk about how my boyfriend and I were living together but weren't married. I often thought about it, and more so when my mother brought it up. When my boyfriend came home from work one day, I finally brought up what my mother and I had been talking about. I asked him what he thought about us getting married. I said to him, "We are already living together and have a child." He felt he wasn't ready.

I wasn't ready for marriage or living together, either, not to mention being a full-time mother. Life was moving so fast, but I told him we could not live together like we were husband and wife if we were not married. Later that day, my boyfriend came home and said, "Okay, let's do it; let's get married."

Surprise, Surprise

I was so excited and couldn't wait to call my mom. However, when he called his mom to tell her we had decided to get married, his mother was not happy. His mother thought we were too young to be getting married. We were also too young to be a family. His mother and my mother talked about it, and eventually his mother did give us her blessings. We set the date for August 30, the day after his birthday, because he didn't want to celebrate his birthday and wedding anniversary on the same day. He felt his birthday would be lost between the two. At any event, we only had about two months to get ready.

Our mothers started planning the wedding. We started going to counseling. Even though it was up and down at times, seeing we were such a young couple, we still decided to go on with the wedding. Finally, when the day came, I remember getting ready and being nervous. When we got to the church, everyone was waiting inside. My stepdad and I were getting ready in the back, waiting for the doors to open for me to walk down the aisle. I started looking through the windows, and I could see my bridesmaids and his groomsmen, along with the pastor, standing there.

My little brother, who was five years old at the time, was holding the rings, and my older brother had our now eight-month-old daughter sitting in the pew. I turned to my stepdad and said to him, "I'm really getting married" as the doors began to open. The first thing I saw was my soon-to-be husband, standing there, waiting for me to walk down the aisle, looking more handsome the closer I got to him. I started getting more and more nervous as I approached the altar. As the ceremony was going on, my little brother could not stand still while he was holding the rings. Eventually, he dropped the rings and started chasing them all around. It was just about the third time the pastor had asked him to stop moving around and to stand still. Everyone was laughing and thought it was funny, but the pastor didn't think it was funny. So, he made my little brother go sit down.

We were finally ready to say our wedding vows to each other. We both were very nervous. We eventually got through the wedding vows. Then the pastor said, "You may kiss the bride." So, we kissed, and there it was; I was married.

It all happened so fast. I remember thinking to myself, "Wow, I'm Mrs. Sharp." I thought, "How cool is that!" I was now a mother and a wife. I remember my mother telling me she had to sign for me to get married because I hadn't turned eighteen yet. But she never informed me about signing a marriage certificate to validate our marriage. I didn't know at the time that we had to go downtown for her to give me permission and sign the marriage certificate to get married.

The Biggest Mistake

There was a time when I made the biggest mistake of my life. It was when I decided to have a second abortion. God showed me grace and favor when He spared me the first time. I don't know why I would even consider this as an option, seeing how much I love my oldest daughter. I can't even imagine life without her. Now I have to live with this decision for the rest my life. For years, I could not forgive myself. It took a lot of my life away from me, having to live with the thought I took an innocent life. I never talked about it until I gave my life back to the Lord. I know it was my choice.

I felt so bad afterward. I would start throwing up every time I thought about it. There were times when I wouldn't even get out of bed for days. After years of holding it in, I was finally able to tell my daughters when they got older of the terrible mistake I made. I would justify it by saying I was really young. I wanted them to forgive me and hoped they wouldn't judge me or make me feel like I was the worst mother in the world. I wish I would've reached out for advice or gotten the help that was available at the time. This is why I'm sharing this part of my story with you. It's my hope that it will help someone else who may be facing this same heartbreaking decision as they are reading this book.

Encounter with God

What helped me to get over the pain of having an abortion was when I went to an Encounter Retreat with my church. An Encounter is very similar to what most know as a revival. Every year we would go to an Encounter. We would fellowship, worship, and pray. During a certain part of the Encounter, everyone got an opportunity to write down everything they had ever done in the past that may not have been pleasing to God. We got a chance to write down everything we held on to or blamed ourselves for. At the end of the session, we would nail these things on the cross or burn them in a bonfire, which was a large fire built in the open air for warmth, entertainment, and celebration.

This was considered your one-on-one personal time with God. You got the chance to do a lot of soul searching. You were able to get rid of the things that had haunted you for years. I was always too scared to show my feelings, so the burden I was carrying stuck with me. But I do thank God for His mercy and grace. I thank Him for His Son, Jesus Christ, who died on the cross for all of my sins, even when I didn't deserve it. He forgave me for not being perfect.

At the time my mom thought I was too young for another baby. I wanted my husband to tell me it was okay, let's have the baby. However, he didn't think we were ready for another child. The next day, we went together to have the abortion procedure. It was as hard on him as it was on me. We never knew about all the optional support programs that were available to help us through this gut-wrenching, decision-making process.

In the end, I should have followed my own heart. I blamed my husband for years until finally, I came to the realization I had to release him and stop blaming him because of the decision I made. After all, he was just as young as I was. He didn't know, just like I didn't know. I had to learn not to judge him for my mistake.

Back to the Story

When we found out, thirty-five years later, that we were never legally married, it was the most shocking and most devastating news for the both of us. The one thing that I love about my husband is when we found out, he said, "Let's just get remarried and be done with it." He never looked at the situation as being a problem. He just wanted to do what we needed to do to fix the problem. But there was only one catch. I wanted not only to renew our wedding vows, but to have a complete wedding ceremony, with all of my new friends and family. I didn't feel comfortable just going down to city hall and having a random minister come out and say a few words over us, and that would be it. I felt I deserved to have a proper wedding ceremony. My husband was totally against it in the beginning, but, like always, eventually he came around and said yes.

So, I set out on the task of gathering wedding announcements, getting addresses, names, and numbers of close friends and family members, not knowing this would become a monumental task. The first thing I had to do was to find a location for the ceremony. A friend of mine said she and her husband would be honored if we would allow them to host the wedding ceremony in their beautiful backyard. The friends' backyard was about one square acre in size. There was a large area with a pool in the middle of the yard, where the wedding would take place. Ironically, we weren't sure if our own pastor would be available to preside over the wedding. Once our date was set, we found out our pastor had a prior engagement to host an Encounter in the mountains. Just for clarification, an Encounter is similar to a revival.

We were running out of choices when our pastor called and said, "Don't worry about it; I'll be there to perform the ceremony." You talk about taking the weight off my shoulders. I was relieved when he agreed to make arrangements to preside over our wedding. We were supposed to start the wedding procedures at 5:00 p.m. however, we didn't physically start the wedding session until 7:00 p.m. Everyone was really patient, and there was very little complaining. When the pastor got there, we started the ceremony right away. It was perfect. We were really blessed to have a pastor who would cut short a very important event in order to administer our wedding. It showed us his commitment to our family. We, as well as he, were honored the way it all came together.

After the ceremony, we took pictures and ate some good food that was catered in by some of our close church friends. Everyone wanted to help to make this wedding special. While others were eating, a few people got up and spoke eloquently on our behalf. It could not have been a more perfect ending to a beautiful new wedding day.

Chapter 4
Leaving Riverside Behind

The beginning of this story was based on finding out what had happened and why we were never even legally married. This is why I started writing this book. I wanted to tell my story and talk about looking back on how I grew up. When I was growing up in Ontario, California, my mother would tell me stories about why she moved our family out of Riverside. My mother met my dad in Riverside, where she gave birth to me. I was one of four siblings growing up in a household, all raised by a single mother. I never knew my dad except for the stories my mom would tell me about him. One story Mom told me, in particular, which always stuck in my head, was when my mother was at a local Laundromat, washing clothes with me and my older sister.

My mother said my dad pulled up to the Laundromat and could see her inside. So, he parked and came in. She expressed she was really scared of him. She said he came in and instantly started beating her. She mentioned he tried to put her inside one of the dryers. Mom told me she ran out of the Laundromat and started screaming for help. My dad then took me from my mom and said she wasn't getting me back. She had to call the police, telling them my father had just beaten her up and taken me from her. I was only six months old at the time. When she called the police department, they sent the helicopters and fire department to his sister's house. The police made my dad bring me out of his sister's house where he was holding me. Mom said when I saw her, I jumped out of his arms and into hers.

After the whole ordeal was over, my father said to my mother, "Riverside isn't big enough for the both of us," so my mother decided to leave Riverside. Mom packed everything she owned in the car, along with, me, my sister, and my brothers, and off we went. Momma said she had to have the police escort her to the freeway. Mom said it was at that very moment she realized she had to leave Riverside for good.

After Momma left Riverside, she never looked back. She always told me how scared and afraid she was of my father, mainly because of how violent he was. Mom did acknowledge that my father, at one point, was a handsome and caring man who made a living working in construction. Momma mentioned to me that Dad was always nice to her while she was pregnant. He bought her nice maternity clothes and was very attentive to all of her needs. He would always buy her nice things. As a matter of fact, the day I was born, Momma said my dad walked into the hospital and paid the full hospital bill in cash. In those days, you had to pay your bill in full. But soon after I was born, he went right back to violently beating her. Mom said my dad was a very jealous man, so it didn't take much to set him off.

The funny thing is, I had only heard these stories from my mom's perspective. I really wanted to know more and to see if everything my mother said about my father was true. So, when I turned eighteen, I went to Riverside, looking for my dad. I wanted to know if my dad was the type of man my mother described him to be.

Not knowing what to expect, I drove to Riverside to find my dad. When I got to Riverside, I went to a local bar, where my mother said Dad had spent a lot of his time drinking with the guys back in the day. I walked in and started asking, "Does anyone know my dad?" When I said his name, as it turned out, a few people knew who he was. As it turned out, a few people knew who he was. I explained who I was, and that I was looking for my dad. Everyone was happy to know why I was looking for him. The people at the bar were more than happy to tell me where he lived.

After getting the information I needed, I went to the address where they told me he lived. It was a trailer home located behind someone else's home. I knocked on the door, and when he opened it, he smiled right at me like he knew who I was. The first question I asked him was, "Are you my father?" First, he smiled, and then he reached into his pocket and pulled out an old wallet. Inside of his wallet was a picture that had a baby on it. It was the same baby picture my mother had given me. I knew then he was my dad.

We sat down in front of his trailer and talked for a while. And true enough, a lot of the things Momma had told me were sadly true. My dad could not really explain his behavior, but he did confess he loved my mother. Sometimes love will make you do some crazy things. As the evening started to grow dark, we made a promise to continue seeing each other and getting to know one another.

Remember, I was only six months old at the time we moved. But, through it all, he always said, "She was a beautiful lady," and that's just how he was. Momma continued to stress how afraid of him she was. In fact, my mother admitted she was still afraid of him eighteen years later. I asked Mom if she would be willing to go with me one particular time. After much encouraging, she finally agreed to go with me. My dad and I decided we would meet at one of the local small-town restaurants in Riverside. Momma was extremely nervous, not knowing what to expect.

I had to tell my mom, "He can't hurt you anymore." He was just a big old, mean, jealous man. In fact, he was literally big in his physical stature. He was a big, burly man with big hands that were like bear claws. His nails were thick, with cracks and splits in them. He was around six feet, two inches tall. He weighed around 270 pounds. He had a couple of patches of hair, along with a few bald spots. One thing I also noticed was that my dad didn't have any teeth in his mouth. So, when we ordered lunch, I asked him, "How do you eat without teeth?" He said he actually ate better with no teeth than he did when he had teeth.

When we started eating, Mom just sat there, keeping her distance and being aware of anything that might set him off again. Momma wasn't comfortable in his presence. We spent the next two hours talking and eating. After we finished eating, Momma said she would never come back to visit or be in this man's presence again. The events she went through had really traumatized her and had lasting effects on her.

As the conversation continued, we eventually started talking about why he wouldn't come to see me get married. My dad said he would never leave Riverside again, not even to see me get married. On the day I got married, he gave my cousin a hundred dollars to give to me for a wedding gift. I thought, "For seventeen years I lived in a town that was only thirty minutes away, and he never once tried to find out where I was."

As the years went by, I continued to see him. I eventually took my youngest daughter to meet her grandfather. She wanted to confirm the stories that were told to me by my mother. She couldn't believe I wasn't exaggerating. He didn't deny any of it, right in front of my daughter. He admitted he used to beat my mother. He acknowledged, saying, "Riverside wasn't big enough for the both of us." He also said he didn't pay child support because of how hurt he was because Momma had called the police on him. He was hurt because not only did the police come out, but also police helicopters and the fire department came to his sister's house.

The second time my daughter and I went to see her grandfather, we pulled up to his sister's house, who is my aunt. When we got out of the car, to both of our amazement, Dad was standing next to a cage with a possum inside of it. I asked him, "Why do you have a possum in a cage?" Dad said he had just caught it and was going to make possum stew out of it. He also had some little chickens, running around in the front yard. Dad wanted to give my daughter one of the chickens, but my daughter couldn't even think about the chicken because she was more scared of the possum in the cage.

Dad's Confession

As we continued to talk, out of the clear blue sky, Dad began to tell us he was sick. Dad revealed to us he had been diagnosed with terminal cancer. He expressed to me, if he were to die today, he really didn't care if his family just threw him in the trash and were done with it. My daughter looked at him and then at me. I said, "Why would you say something like that?" He said he really didn't care about anything, and pretty much, they could do whatever they wanted to after he was dead and gone. Those comments saddened me that he felt that way. It made me wonder what had been going on in his life that he would take a position such as that.

After moving to Fresno years later, I got a call from Riverside Community Hospital, saying my father was in the hospital and requesting to see me. The hospital noted my dad was really sick. They told me if I wanted to see him, I didn't have much time, so my husband and I got in the car the next day and drove from Fresno directly to Riverside Community Hospital. While we were driving, about halfway into the drive, I got another phone call from the hospital, saying I needed to safely get there as fast as I could.

Finally getting there, we walked into the hospital, trying to find out what room he was in and what floor he was on. Once getting into the elevator, we started to go up. When the door opened, we were on the fourth floor. As we began to walk out of the elevator and into the hallway, a nurse met us and asked if I was the daughter of the man who was in the same room I was headed to.

She said my father just passed away and gave me her deepest condolence. The nurse continued by saying how sorry she was for my loss. Tears started rolling down my face as we walked into the room. He was lying in the bed; the nurse and my husband left the room. I sat on the bed next to him, looking at my father's face, still warm. A tear rolled down from his eye while I sat, looking at him. I laid my head on his chest and said, "I love you, Dad, and I forgive you." I never would have thought I would be the one who would be there when my dad died or have to be the one who would bury him.

Chapter 5
Losing Mom

Twelve short years later, my mom passed away. I was at work when my daughter called me crying and saying, "Momma, Grandma passed away."

I said, "Nooooo, it can't be true, not my mom." Feeling sick to my stomach, I started crying out of control. I walked outside from my job, got in my car, and left work and never went back to work at that facility. I just drove home, crying in my car. When I got home, I just crawled into my bed, crying uncontrollably. Eventually, my brother called and said Mom had passed away. I lay there feeling numb. I was broken, after receiving a call no one ever wants to receive.

Later I learned the doctor had found cancer in her colon while doing a routine colon check. So, my mom was scheduled for surgery to have the cancer removed. Once the cancer was removed, the doctor said he had gotten it all. So, we all thought she was going to get better, but the cancer came back and grew even larger, moving into her abdomen. So, a second surgery was scheduled. This time, it was for a full hysterectomy.

We were sure the doctor removed all of the cancer. Momma tried to fight to get better for almost a year, but the cancer and radiation were too much. She remained in a lot of pain from the scars that were growing in her abdomen. It was very painful for me to see the pain she was in.

Before my mom passed, she called me and said, "You don't love me anymore."

I said, "Mom, why would you say that? I've always loved you." I truly think that was her way of wanting to hear me tell her, for the last time, I loved her.

During this whole process, I believe my sister didn't tell me or my brothers how sick Momma really was. She kept everything from the family of the painful inevitable outcome, which was Momma was dying. I got a call from my sister telling me, in her words, "You need to catch the next train smoking and get here as soon as you can."

I asked her, "What are you saying? What's going on with Momma?"

"Your mother is dying," my sister said.

I said, "What do you mean she's dying? I thought the doctor said he got all the cancer during the first surgery?"

I immediately drove back home to Pomona for Momma's second surgery. When I got into town, I went directly to the hospital. Just as I got to the hospital, the doctors were bringing Momma out of surgery. My sister and I were right there as she came out of surgery. As Momma opened her big brown eyes, she looked at me and said, "Where are my daughters?"

We said, "Right here, Momma," and I said, "I love you, Mom," as she closed her eyes to sleep.

I wanted so badly for my mom to get better after the surgery. She really tried to give it her all. I always knew growing up, I would be there when that time came. Living in Fresno was hard, for me to live away from my mom. We talked every day on the phone, sometimes two to three times a day. I went home for vacations as much as I could in order to be with my mom.

At one point, Momma even moved to Fresno to be close to me. I was so happy that my stepdad and my two nieces came along with her. However, Momma did move back home after several years. It made me really sad. Momma didn't realize I had a family to take care of. It seemed like I saw Momma less in Fresno than I did when she lived back in Pomona because I was working all the time and taking the kids to their sports practices and games. My husband was busy coaching high school sports and working a full-time teaching job. I should have held on to her a little longer. Momma still came back to visit when she could.

I remember Momma called me while she was living with my sister, after getting out of the hospital and going through her treatments, and said to me that she was not happy being there. I called my stepdad and asked him to bring her to me. I wanted to take care of my mom, but she was just too weak to travel. Eventually, Mom did get her own apartment. My mom called me after several weeks and said, "I'm walking now."

I said, with hope in my heart, "Good, Mom; you continue fighting. As soon as you get better, we'll go on a trip—just you and me."

She said, "Why do we have to wait?"

I mentioned to her, we didn't have to wait. I said, "Momma, I just want you to be strong enough to travel."

Sad to say, we never got the chance. Days later, my brother called and began to explain how our mother passed away. He said they were taking her to the restroom, which was down the hallway. As they were going down the hallway, she stopped and said, "What was that?" My brother said she closed her eyes and fell to the ground. My other brother, who was also helping Mom to the restroom, was right there while my brother, who called me with the news of Mom passing away, tried to give her CPR until the ambulance got there. She passed away on her way to the hospital.

Four months prior to Mom's passing, my family and I drove down to Upland, California, to visit her. I remember Momma wanting me to wash her hair over her kitchen sink and give her a few braids. She was trying her best to lean over the sink, to lower her head under the water faucet. It broke my heart to see my mom in such pain from the aftereffects of going through her cancer surgeries and treatments.

I remember my husband asking Momma if she knew the sinner's prayer, quoting Romans 10:9 that says, "That if you confess with your mouth that Jesus is Lord and believe in your heart that God rose from the dead, you will be saved." Also, he told her Romans 10:10 continues by saying, "For with the heart, one believes resulting in righteousness; and with the mouth confession is made resulting in salvation." My husband made sure she said the sinner's prayer with him. Momma confessed she loved that her son-in-law was a minister.

On the same day we were leaving to go back to Fresno, as we were driving away, Momma was standing in the doorway of her apartment, looking directly at me, and I was looking directly at her. There was a feeling in the air I couldn't explain. But for some reason, it felt like it was going to be the last time I would see her. I think my family could also sense what I was feeling, as my family was sad as well. I was looking at her face with such sadness while tears were coming down my face. I was trying to hide it from my family, but in reality, I couldn't. I didn't want to leave. In my heart it was like we both knew it was the last time we were going to see each other.

Ironically, when she passed, it was my daughter who said to me, "Mom, be strong, and keep your faith in God. He will see you through." My daughter knew that her grandma was in heaven, looking down on me. My daughter reminded me that Grandma loved me very much and was also very proud of me. My daughter also reminded me that Grandma would want me to remember what she did her entire life for others, which was opening her door to those who knew her.

Even after all of the consoling from my daughter and the rest of the family, I still went through a deep depression for a while. I shut down and started having anxiety attacks. I started going to the doctor's office and running to the emergency hospital about once a week. One particular time, my husband went with me, and as we went to the back room to be seen, an African American nurse came into the room. She took one look at me and said, "I don't know why you're here; you don't need anything here." She said, "All you need is Jesus."

Immediately, something came over me, as my husband and I looked at each other and said she was right. I got up and looked back at the nurse and said, "You know what? You're right." I truly believe that nurse was an angel sent from heaven to help me overcome my anxiety.

Adversaries

When I was growing up, I wanted to be just like my big sister. I noticed she was kind of cool for a big sister. However, just about the time I was turning fifteen, I started to notice our relationship was changing. My sister started to treat me differently. I was starting to grow into who I would become as a teenager. My body started to change. I started to fill out. It seemed like my sister started getting jealous of me.

It was hard for me because we never really got along. At first, I had a little respect for her when I was younger. But as the years went by, our relationship got pretty bad. I never understood why she always had a problem with me. I thought she was the worst person. I hated her because she was always mean to me, always trying to provoke me into fighting. I didn't even want to be around her.

There was no trust, no respect, and no love, just hatred and jealousy. When I started growing up and becoming a teenager, that's when a lot of it started. When Mom passed away, my sister finally said she hated the fact we all grew up to have our own personal relationships with Mom. It made her jealous of each of us. She confessed this to me, right after Mom passed away. So, I forgave her, thinking she was hurting from the passing of our mother.

Sometimes people's real emotions come out whenever they experience a hardship in their life. I could understand how she might have felt, being she was the oldest and having to do everything for us growing up. It was a huge responsibility. You feel as though your youth is being taken away from you when you have to grow up and take on responsibilities that are not your own. Even with this being the case, she never changed; it only got worse. I've tried, all my life, to understand my sister. I would forgive her every time we had a problem. Don't get me wrong; I still loved my sister, even though we didn't always get along.

Chapter 6
Mom's Funeral

When Mom passed away, my uncle wrote the most beautiful poem ever. It talked about having to let her go. It talked about not being selfish, wanting to keep her and hold on to her, even though she was suffering and in pain. It talked about the wonderful person she was. Lastly, it talked about seeing her again in heaven. It brought tears to everyone's eyes who was there. I remember the whole church being filled. There were people from all walks of life there to celebrate Mom's home-going service. Blacks, whites, Mexicans, Asians, Indians--you name it, they were there. But this didn't surprise me at all. You see, Mom was just that type of person. She had love for everyone, and everyone had love for her. Everyone knew who the queen was.

There, in the same room were three of my brothers' fathers. Two of the fathers were ministers, and one was her husband. During the funeral service, my sister had to go and get my stepfather from standing at the door to come in and sit down. It was really hard for him to be there and deal with his fear of death. Just the thought of our mom having to fight for her life and then her passing away was just too much for him to bear.

Taking a Look Back In Order to Move Forward

Even for me, Mom's funeral was the hardest thing I ever had to deal with in my life. You cannot really understand what it's like until you have to bury your mother. We all know one day we will die. Hebrews 9:27 says it this way: "And as it is appointed unto men once to die." The Bible also tells us in Matthew 24:36 that no man knows the day or the hour when these things will happen, not even the angels in heaven or the Son Himself. Only the Father knows. Every day we seem to get up and do the same thing. We wake up, get our day started, and then we come home, maybe cook dinner, and then prepare for the next day. This can become routine for most of us. We're never really prepared for that one call we never want to receive.

As for the three fathers who were there, I saw tears and sadness in their faces. I know all three of them loved Mom in their own way, at one time or another. I know if she could have looked down from heaven and seen all three of them in the same room together, not arguing or fighting, she would have said, "Look at God; won't He do it?" She would have been very pleased.

The funeral service was packed with all of mom's grandkids, nieces and nephews, cousins, all of mom's sons and daughters, sons-in-law, daughters-in-law, close friends, and friends of friends. I clearly remember like it was yesterday that the funeral service was standing room only. Every seat was taken. There were people standing all over the place. There were people who had to wait outside because they couldn't get in. This was a true testament of how much Mom was loved.

I remember having to sit up front with the family, and I was staring at Mom. They should've closed the casket at the beginning of the service, but for some strange reason, they didn't. I was staring so much, thinking this would be the last time ever seeing my mother's face. I stared so long and hard that my husband kept telling me to not get fixated on Mom's face. He didn't want it to become a look I could never get out of my head. It was hard because I just tuned him out for a long while before I finally stopped staring. But while I was staring, I couldn't help but think, actually, how good Mom looked. Mom looked as though she were sleeping, not a worry or stress in her face. You could see she wasn't in any pain. She had the glory of God all over her.

Although my sister and I don't always get along, the one thing I can say is my sister did a good job in putting the funeral service together. She and my niece did such a beautiful job with our mom. I can honestly say how good Mom looked, and for that, I give my sister respect. She was the only one strong enough to gracefully plan and do the funeral. What I mean by being strong enough is that my sister and niece dressed Mom and put on her makeup. I personally could not have done it. I know me; I would've been a mess.

Missing You

I knew I'd been scarred for a lifetime, when my mom passed away. You see, Mom was the backbone of our family. It's been ten years since Mom's passing, yet I can still remember it like it was yesterday. I still feel as if I have not fully recovered from the trauma of losing her. My relationship with my mom was one of the best relationships a mother and daughter could possibly share. Mom was truly my best friend. We always talked on the phone every day and sometimes two or three times a day. Mom was really funny. She could make me laugh, even on my worst of days.

Mom was always there for me. As I take a look back, I remember before Mom died, she told me to stop arguing and try to get along with my husband. Mom said, "Life is too short," as she was a living testament to her very words, lying there sick. I made a promise to Mom that I would do better. Even to this day, I tell myself, "I can do better." I can be a better wife. I can be a better mother. I can be a better friend. I can choose my words better. I can make better choices in my life. Simply, I can do better.

I Had a Dream

On this one particular night, I had a dream about my mom. It was the first time I dreamed about her since her passing away. In the dream, I was driving in a car. Momma was holding on to the back of the car. I don't know how or why this was taking place. I was saying to my mother, as I continued to look back at her, "Hold on, Mom, hold on." My mom started saying, "It's okay. I'm all right. You don't have to worry about me anymore. I'm all right, now. I'm not in any more pain. The only pain I have is the pain of seeing you stress out over me, wondering if I'm okay." When I woke up, my eyes were burning from crying in my dream. The dream did, however, give me confirmation that Momma was all right and in heaven. I could let go now and not have to worry anymore. Now that I knew this, it gave me comfort to move on and live my life in peace.

Chapter 7
Family Letters

Over the years, as my daughters got older, they would give me cards and letters expressing their love for me. As they got older, it was harder for my oldest daughter to express her emotion toward me. So, one day she wrote me a beautiful letter. Sometimes it's hard for her to express her feelings, and she really hasn't figured out why. My oldest daughter mentioned she knew she had these expressions of love, but despite it, it was hard for her to just say it out loud. So, she wanted to write this letter to me.

Mom, because of that very reason, I love you so much it hurts sometimes. I try to control my feelings by doing other things, not involving myself with what has gotten me so emotional in the first place. Most of the time, I don't know the reason I express my affection the way I do. It may not be the right way all the time, but for now, reading between the lines will have to do.

I'm in this place in my life where I'm trying to find my way, and the road gets a little bumpy at times. I need some reassurance along the way.

What I'm trying to say to you is you mean the world to me. I'm honored you were chosen to be my mother. I have loved you with every breath in my body and every beat in my heart. Life without you seems not to exist.

Second, I'm most fond of a sister whom I adore as my guardian angel. Third, I am blessed to have a loving father who adores his daughters, and a hardworking mother who bore a family from the sweat of her tears and the blood of her fingers. Mom, if you don't get it by now or even understand what it is I'm trying to say, let me spell it out for you. You are the mother of my dreams. I deeply love you.

My youngest daughter also wrote a letter, saying it was really encouraging to her to see me overcome the trials and adversities that were tormenting me and giving me anxiety, and the trials and adversities of not knowing who I was. She said, *"I can honestly say, I don't know what I would do without you or Dad."* She told me to always dream big, never take no for an answer, and remember, everything is negotiable, even rent. My daughter went on to say, *"You and Grandma always had a great relationship."* Lastly, she offered, *"Grandma would be proud of the mother, wife, and businesswoman you've become."* When she said that, it broke me down because I always wanted to make Mom proud of me.

My husband wrote a cute letter saying, "To be used only in a case of burning desire." His card had a picture of a fire truck and a fireman on the front of it. The fireman had a fire extinguisher in his hand. The caption read, "There's no cooling me down when you're around."

He wrote: *"I know things have been a trip lately for the both of us, but we're both working hard to have nice things in life. We really need to work together to help make each other's dreams come true. It really doesn't work when we're being petty about our relationship. We both have feelings, so we need to try and respect each other. I know we argue over little things, but all in all, I do love you—and only you."*

Daughter's Father's Day Card

My firstborn was born prematurely at six months. She weighed only four pounds and measured only eighteen inches long. She stayed in the hospital for a few extra days. The hospital had a nurse come to my house for two weeks after she was born to make sure she was doing okay. After the two weeks, everything was going fine, so the hospital released her from their care.

As she began to grow, I remember buying her first baby jacket. It was the cutest little jacket. It was so small you could put a baby toy doll in it. As I look back, I still have the jacket put up in my keepsakes treasure chest, along with all the other things my two daughters have given me as mementos as they were growing up.

The Father's Day card was really special because this is when my daughters started to express themselves emotionally. I was able to see that they were able to express their emotions and explain what their emotions meant to them. As my firstborn was growing up, she made a Father's Day card for her dad, called "Dad's Life Story." She wrote on the card some of the things she vividly remembered about her dad. She noted when he would go over to my mother's house, how her dad would take me to different places, like the movies, sporting events, the fair, the park, different parties, basketball events, and so on.

She wrote on the card how Dad and Mom became more and more in love. Because their love grew stronger and stronger, soon Dad and Mom got married. After marriage, they had one daughter, and soon after there was another daughter, her sister. Now there was a whole family called the Sharp family.

Dad began to go to college, and in college, Dad played even more basketball. Mom started a cleaning business. Now it was Father's Day. My daughter wanted to express to her dad how much she loved him. She felt saying "I love you, Dad," just wasn't enough. So, she, to the best of her recollection, made a card with a family timeline on it. The card had a lot of great memories on it, such as memories of being potty trained and memories of squeezing her navel, thinking it was the way to pee because she had seen her dad standing up and peeing over the urinal. There were memories of when she first started school. She remembered all the Halloween costumes she wore when we took her trick-or-treating. She recalled great memories of visiting her godmother.

She also added some memories of all the times we went to the movies in her dad's old Buick Skylark and how she and her sister would get on top of the car and watch the movies. Or, when Dad would park the car backward and lay the seats down and let up the hatchback. There were memories of learning to ride a bike for the first time and memories of learning how to fish for the first time. She added memories of playing school and wanting to be a teacher because her dad was a teacher. Finally, she added memories of playing sports for the first time. All of these memories were in her dad's Father's Day card.

Chapter 8
Finger Injury

Because I clean houses for a living, I decided to take a class in order for me to carry a concealed weapon. You see, sometimes I would get a call to do an estimate on a prospective client's home, and when I would get to the prospective client's home, there would only be a man there. It made me feel very uncomfortable. I vowed I would never allow myself to be in that type of situation again. So, I decided to take a weapons class. I took a carrying-a-concealed-weapon (CCW) class, where you get a license to carry a handgun once you successfully complete the class. Once I completed the class and background check, I was able to legally carry a gun with me.

It was around the Fourth of July. My daughter, husband, and I, along with several members of the church, had been working a fireworks booth for a fund-raiser for the church we attended. On this particular night, after finishing our shift and coming home as we usually did, I went into my bedroom, and I sat my purse down on the floor against the wall. I reached into my purse to remove my gun, as I did every night. On this night, though, upon my taking the gun out of my purse, it fired and exploded at the same time in my hand.

I looked down and dropped the gun. I felt a ringing feeling in my hand. As I looked at my hand, there was blood everywhere. Once I got past the shock of all the blood, I noticed my index finger was split down the middle and was bleeding pretty badly. I yelled out to my husband, "I shot myself." My husband was in the living room, and my daughter was in her bedroom, when they heard a loud popping sound. My husband came running into the room.

The first thing I said was, "Let's go." I quickly went down the hallway to my daughter's room and told her what had just happened. She came back into my room and saw all the blood; it was everywhere. She tried putting a bandage on my finger. I don't know what I was thinking at the time, trying to put a bandage on an open wound like that. Of course, this was not working, so my daughter was trying to clean up the blood, as we were getting ready to go to the hospital's emergency room.

I was in shock. My husband put his clothes on as fast as he could, and we got right into the car and drove to the hospital's emergency room. When we got there, I was admitted right away, due to the nature of my injury. As I mentioned earlier, I was still in shock.

When they took me back into the hospital area where they would take a look at my finger, there was an officer present. The officer started asking questions while looking at my husband. As we tried to explain to him it was a gunshot accident, the officer questioned my husband because he thought it may have been a domestic violence incident. I explained to the officer my husband wasn't even in the room when the gun went off. My husband said he was glad he wasn't in the room because of the way the officer kept trying to place him in the room and thinking it was a domestic violence situation.

By this time the nurse had come into the room to check on my injured finger. When the nurse saw the injury, she said, "Wow, that's a nasty injury." She gave me a shot right into my finger to numb it. After the shot, the nurse started cleaning out the wound. She had to clean out all the gunpowder burn. She thought it would only need stitches, but then she said, "We're going to send you to a hand specialist because of how bad the wound looks."

I remember having to wait to see the specialist because the injury happened on a Friday and I had to wait until Monday to see the specialist. When I got to the specialist's office, the first thing he asked me was, "What happened?" I began to explain to him what had happened, while he was looking at my finger. He explained to me what had to be done in order to get my hand back to as close to 100 percent as possible. The specialist said I would need surgery because the explosion had blown out the nerve, and some of the skin had disintegrated.

First, I would need surgery to repair the nerve. Second, I would also need to have a skin graft to repair the disintegrated skin. The specialist explained to me he would remove a nerve from my hand to put into my finger. He went on to say the skin graft would require him to connect both my index finger and middle finger together, so the nerve would grow back in straight. This procedure was called a flap. It would be done, using a screw and staples. Third, I would take injections to remove as much of the scar tissue as possible on my hand and fingers. Last of all, the specialist said

I would need a lot of therapy to regain strength back into my hand.

The bullet hole is still in my bedroom wall. As I think back, this situation could have been a lot worse than it was. Although I will have these scars for the rest of my life, I am thankful, in the end, it didn't turn out any worse than it did. I truly believe God's grace was watching over me.

Chapter 9
The Dog

I never wanted a dog. I always thought dogs were messy and would be a big responsibility. On one particular Christmas, my husband thought he would surprise me and get me a dog. He felt if I would ever accept a dog, Christmas would be the perfect time. Mind you, I had told him for years that I did not ever want a dog. Some friends of ours had dogs that were having puppies, so my husband thought this was a good opportunity to get a dog. The dog was a beautiful Akita breed. My husband thought the timing was perfect. Not only was he getting a dog from our friends, but the dog was from a beautiful breed. He didn't want to bring home a mutt with no pedigree.

My husband left the dog at our friend's house until the last day to pick her up because he knew how I would respond to him once he brought the dog home. Diamond, what we eventually named her, was only six weeks old at the time. My husband and daughter were trying to surprise me. I remember later calling the friend whom he got the dog from, telling her how mad I was because she didn't tell me what was going on. On Christmas Day, my husband and daughter left to go pick the dog up.

When they got back, I was just opening the door as they were pulling up. I looked outside, and I saw the dog in a small cage. The dog was all white with a red bow and red collar. As they were getting out of the car with the dog, my husband was trying to hide the cage to surprise me, but it was too late. I had already seen the cage. I remember looking at my husband as he was bringing the dog into the house. I said, "I know that's not a dog!" I said it a second time, "I know that's not a dog!" I said, "It's not coming in here." My husband and daughter looked at me as he brought the dog into the house. I said "No, it's not staying here." I was beside myself and out of control.

My mom and stepdad just happened to be visiting from Pomona for Christmas. My mother said, "Calm down."

I said, "No, it's either me or the dog. I don't want a dog. I don't care what you do with that dog, but you better take it somewhere else." My husband didn't know what to say or do with the dog. He was looking at me like I was crazy. I said, "It's either me or the damn dog." But this time I said it with a lot more authority. My husband saw I was serious and started to realize there was a possibility he would have to get rid of the dog. My husband started to call to see if someone wanted to take the dog.

Later that day, we had the biggest argument. I was a hot mess, figuratively speaking. For the next few days, my husband was still trying to find someone to take the puppy. During this time, we mainly kept the dog in the garage and outside on the backyard patio. The dog would be looking through the patio door. I would

The Dog

come home and close the blinds so I didn't have to see the dog.

However, on one particular day, I stopped to look at the dog and said to myself, "She is kind of cute." She was all white with big paws. I went to the sliding door to let her into the house. As soon as I opened the sliding door, she ran in right away. She was jumping all over the place in a matter of seconds. I started falling in love with her instantly. I think the feeling was mutual. She actually made me smile and laugh as she started rolling around like a little white baby polar bear. I couldn't believe it myself. I was in love with her already. My husband and I still laugh about it to this day, every time we tell this story.

Years later, I thought we lost her when she got out of the backyard gate. My daughter and I went looking for her. We drove around the whole neighborhood. After not being able to find her, I was heartbroken. I thought we had lost her. When we got back home, we were hoping she had found her way back to the house. When we got home, we started calling her name. This time, she came running right to us. She was in the backyard the whole time, on the other side of the house. I was so happy. It's funny how I went from not wanting the dog to not being able to do without the dog. And to think, this dog almost cost me my whole marriage.

It's laughable how I went from not wanting the dog to paying thousands of dollars for her medical bills. There were a couple of time when she got really sick. One time in particular, she lost a lot of weight. She kept throwing up and wouldn't eat for days. I knew it was bad when I came outside one afternoon, and she was in the backyard, lying under the peach tree. They say when a dog is about to die, they will go away from people and crawl off into a corner somewhere and die. I remember calling her name, then calling her a second time, and still, she would not come. I thought she had gotten out again. The last time I called her, with a forceful voice, she raised her head up, and I could see she was under the peach tree. Diamond could barely move. When she slowly came from under the tree, I said to myself, "Something's wrong."

I immediately, along with my husband, put Diamond into the car and took her to the emergency veterinarian, right down the street from where we live. Clearly there was something wrong. When we got there, within minutes the veterinarian took Diamond into the back. Minutes later, the veterinarian (vet) came out and said he would have to perform an emergency operation. We were in shock. The vet informed us that Diamond had a hole in her intestine, and her bile was spilling out inside of her. This is why she couldn't eat. The vet also informed us this emergency procedure would cost around twelve hundred dollars, which we really didn't have. The last thing he mentioned to us was we would have to pay half up front before he could start the operation.

We paid the six hundred dollars, and the vet performed the operation. When the vet came out of the operating room, he said he was able to delicately stitch her intestine together. He said if Diamond made it through the night, she would have a good chance of making it. The vet told us to hope for the best. We were like, "A good chance of making it?" "Hope for the best?" We were saying to ourselves, "She better make it after all the money we spent." We were also told they would have to keep Diamond overnight to monitor her vitals.

As we walked out of the veterinarian's office, tears started rolling down from my eyes. I was feeling really bad for Diamond. My husband and I went home and waited for the vet's call. It felt so strange not having Diamond there. We were trying to imagine what it would be like without Diamond. We just couldn't wrap our minds around the thought she wouldn't make it. The next morning, we received a call from the vet, informing us that Diamond was doing fine, and she was on her way to a full recovery. I was so grateful the veterinarian saved Diamond's life.

Chapter 10
When You Don't Listen to Your Mother

My mother would always have a saying like, "Don't leave this apartment when I'm gone." But of course, we would always sneak out anyway. I remember one time walking over to my cousin's house to ride the two-wheeler bike she got for her birthday. I couldn't wait to ride it, so I defied my mother's saying and went anyway. I knew all I had to do was to get home before my mom got home, and it would be all good. However, while walking home, I got hit by a car. When I woke up, I was lying in a hospital bed. My left leg was attached to something holding it straight up in the air. My mom and brother were standing there when the doctor walked into the room to explain to all of us what had happened. The doctor explained I had been hit by a car. He also explained that I was lucky to be alive.

As I looked up, I could see Momma crying. Barely able to talk, I said, "Momma, I'm sorry for leaving the apartment. I'm sorry for disobeying you." The doctor said my femur bone was broken in half. I was placed in something that looked like a sling. The medical term for this so-called sling was called traction. I could not get out of bed. I had to spend the next six months in the hospital with my leg in traction. I couldn't wear any clothes at all. The only thing they had me wear was one of those hospital gowns with the open back.

I stayed in the hospital for six months before I got released. Finally, the day before I got out of the hospital, the doctor said I would be placed in a full body cast. This was done so the new bone in my leg would grow in straight. The doctor also mentioned to my mother that there was a possibility I would never be able to have kids. Being only ten years old at that time, I could not really comprehend what the doctor was saying. But my mother fully understood what he was saying. We put this thought out of our mind for the time being. My mother was just happy I was all right and was coming home.

Coming Home

I remember pulling up to our apartment, which we called the housing project. These were apartments for low-income families. My friends, who also lived in the housing project, were waiting anxiously to see me as Mom and I drove up. My friends were all standing outside, not knowing what to expect, waiting for me to come home that day. I know this may sound strange, but I didn't know what to expect either. As Mom and I pulled up in the parking lot, my friends were happy to see me. They started singing this dumb song about me coming home.

After a couple of weeks of being home, I learned how to run and play with my body cast on. At first, my family had to do everything for me. Remember the apartment complex I mentioned earlier? Because they were low-income project-style apartments, most were upstairs-downstairs living arrangements. On one particular day, I remember my brother was trying to carry me down the stairs when he dropped me. I went sliding down the stairs, in my full body cast, all the way down to the bottom of the staircase. I remember laughing the whole time. Although it was fun, I was really lucky I didn't get hurt.

Finally, the day came to get my cast off. Because I had a body cast on for several months, once it was time to take the cast off, one leg was bigger than the other. I had to go through therapy and learn how to walk all over again. Thank God, it all worked out.

Back Down Memory Lane

As a little girl, I used to love playing dress up. I would always put on my mom's clothes and her wigs. When my mom was younger, in the seventies wigs were the thing most women wore. You were able to change up your look without having to spend a lot of money. I loved the way Mom could have a big Afro wig one day, and then the next day she could wear a short wig look.

My favorite was her big Afro wig and her long dresses. I would try on her wig and dress then look in the mirror and imagine I was Mom. I wanted to look and be just like her. Mom always had this look about her—a look of confidence and sophistication. So, when I would try on her clothes, I would always act like I was someone important.

Mom would put on oldies but goodies, old-school records, with her record player. You know, things are so different today that most people may not even know what a record player is. This particular type of record player had a long arm on one side of it. At the end of the arm, there was a needle sticking out of it. You would put the arm with the needle sticking out of it onto the record. The record was a round plastic disc. But, once you put the needle to the record, it would make music. Mom would play old-school blues songs while the grown folks played cards.

Even today, when I hear these same songs on the radio, it takes me back to those very moments when I would play dress up. It brings back great memories of Mom. I can see her sitting there with her eyes closed and a half smile on her face, enjoying her blues. This may be the reason why I still love old-school music today.

The Fighting Siblings

Looking back on my earlier years growing up as an adolescent, I have so many great memories of my brothers and sister. I remember one time when Momma had to be at work early, and my sister had to watch us, as well as cook dinner for us. So, my sister decided to make chili beans for dinner. My older brother wanted to be in control, so he tried to serve us dinner. My older sister said, "Momma left me in charge, so I'll serve them. You can go sit down." I remember vividly that they started arguing over who was going to serve us. They started to push each other around by the stove.

Then it really got crazy. My sister picked up the whole pot of chili beans and threw it all over the kitchen wall. She then said, "If I'm not serving them, no one is. If I'm not serving, then nobody's going to eat what

I made." I was so mad because I was really hungry. Not realizing the mess she had just made, my sister knew she would have to clean up this gigantic mess. The funny thing about it was she knew she had to clean it up before Momma got home.

On the flip side of this whole debacle, my brother and I couldn't wait to tell Momma when she got home. Most of the time it would've been me telling Momma what went on while she was gone. There was always drama at the house. This time, my brother and I were going to tell Momma what had happened. My brother was happy; for once, he wasn't the one who was getting in trouble.

But it wasn't always the kids with all of the drama. One day when I was coming home from school, my mom and her baby sister, my aunt, were having a huge argument outside of our apartment complex by the trash dumpster. Before I could get close enough to both of them to find out what was going on, they started fighting. Momma was working her over pretty good, so my aunt took off running. I said, "Daaaang." Momma could fight. My aunt was so mad when it came down to my mom and her fighting that she told all of her kids not to let us into her apartment anymore.

But of course, every time she was gone, my cousins would let us in. We knew all we had to do was be out of the apartment before our aunt got home. We always went over there to hang out and eat cereal. Auntie always bought the best cereal. So, the next day we were at Auntie's apartment, hanging out with our cousins, eating cereal at the kitchen table. All of a sudden, we heard keys jingling at the front door. It was Auntie. My brother and I got up and ran out as fast as we could. We ran out of the back sliding door and jumped over the back fence.

But before I could get all the way over the fence, my auntie saw me. She was furious. My auntie picked up a broom, which was leaning against the wall, and hit my cousin over her head. I was in shock because the broom broke in half from the force of her downward thrust. She started yelling at my cousin, "I thought I said not to let them damn kids in my house!" Once I heard that, I got over that fence so fast and ran all the way home, not stopping one time.

On another occasion when we lived next to my mom's older sister, my mom and aunt were having a crazy argument about how my mom would allow us kids to just run around, all wild and out of control, while playing. Momma got so mad, she went outside and picked up a brick and threw it through my aunt's glass sliding door. There was a loud explosion and shattered glass everywhere. Everybody was like, wow, what just happened here?

I never knew why there was always fighting going on in my family. My auntie never wanted us kids in the house. She would always say, "Y'all kids go outside and play. You don't need to be all up in grown-folk business." It was like she was always telling that to me the most. I always thought Auntie was the meanest person ever.

However, later I found out she was dying from cancer. I never considered this could have been one of the reasons she always seemed mad at us. She had a reason to be mad, hurt, confused, scared, and all of the above. None of us realized what was going on with her. I remember talking to her when she was alive. She was still worried why everybody in her family was fighting each other when she was the one sick. She just wanted us all to get along and take care and love one another. Here it was, we were fighting and wasting God's gift called life, and my auntie was fighting for her life, metaphorically speaking. I can clearly remember sitting down with my aunt and hearing her say, "I don't want to die." That was our last time talking to each other. She passed shortly after that conversation. It broke my heart.

Chapter 11
Commodity Food

Before I met my boyfriend, I grew up in Ontario. We lived in some apartments called the Duds. They were a low-income family-housing apartment complex for families on welfare. I remember my mom signing up for a government program that gave out food in boxes. We called the food "commodity food." Most families in the apartment complex received commodity food. Everyone knew your family got commodity food because it came in big silver cans. It had a picture of a pig or chicken printed on the can. This is how you knew what was in the can. If it had a pig on the can, then there was chopped pork in the can. If it had a picture of a chicken, then the can had chopped chicken inside of it.

Then there were these really big bags of beans. The bags were at least ten-pound bags. It seemed like you never ran out of beans. Families also got a huge block of cheese, which everyone knew was government cheese. You could do everything with this cheese. You could cut slices and put it on your sandwich. You could make grilled cheese sandwiches, although it seemed like the cheese would never completely melt. You could grate the cheese and put it over the beans Mom would cook. You could slice it and eat it with crackers.

Last of all, there was peanut butter in a can. The peanut butter seemed like it never went bad. You would always have to stir it because of the peanut butter oil it would produce. The peanut butter was so thick that it would make your mouth stick together, and it would tear your bread when you tried to spread it. I remember when I would make peanut butter and white corn syrup sandwiches. Although it was food from the government, we were able to make just about everything--grilled cheese sandwiches, chicken tacos, pork sandwiches, and peanut butter and syrup sandwiches. The cheese was everybody's favorite because of all the ways you could use it.

Sometimes I would open the kitchen cabinet, and there would be all these silver cans in it. I would open up the refrigerator, and there would be these silver cans and a big long block of cheese, so we would know it was the day we had gotten our government commodity food.

Thanksgiving and Christmas

There was one Thanksgiving when Mom came home with a live chicken and duck. She told my brothers to go in the backyard and wring their necks, pluck their feathers, and clean and gut them for Thanksgiving. Mom assumed my brothers would know how to wring the two birds' necks because she had watched her parents and grandparents prepare their chickens and ducks this way when she was a little girl growing up in Arkansas.

I remember watching my brothers from my mom's upstairs bedroom window. My brothers were trying to wring their necks for what seemed like hours. My brothers were trying everything from throwing rocks at the bird, shaking them by their necks, and throwing them to the ground. After all that, no one even wanted to eat the chicken or the duck for Thanksgiving.

Every Christmas in the housing-project apartments, a truck would come around and give out toys. All the kids in the apartment complex would run out to get toys for Christmas. The truck came mainly to the projects where most families were less fortunate. I distinctly remember when the truck arrived, we would all line up, and push and shove each other, trying to be first in line. But like always, there was enough to go around. The funny thing about it, the stuff they gave away was always good quality stuff.

As a family, we never had a lot of money, so my mom would also buy some of our clothes from the Goodwill stores. To my surprise, we would always find some good deals. Most people think when you say Goodwill, there's nothing there but hand-me-downs. Contrary to what others think, people who donate clothes to the Goodwill actually give away some good stuff. In fact, if I would've never told others these clothes were from the Goodwill store, they would've never known.

When I got a little older and started going to high school, I was able to work for a summer jobs' program. The name of the program was called CETA. CETA stood for California Education Training Association. This summer job program allowed low-income students, such as me, to work all summer and earn 1,400 dollars. This was how I was able to start buying my own school clothes, as well as my own school supplies.

A few years later my mom started working for a company call General Dynamics. General Dynamics was an electrical facility that made washers and dryers and refrigerators. Mom worked there for several years until she had a nervous breakdown. Mom eventually went on disability. So, this became our only form of income for years.

Moving on Up

Mom came home one day and said she had met a man, who would eventually become my stepdad. All of a sudden, we started living a lot better than we used to live. Life was starting to look up for our family. Mom, one day, out of the clear blue sky, said, "We're moving."

I remember I started singing this song from the television show called *The Jeffersons*: "Well, we're moving on up, to the East Side. . . . We finally got a piece of the pie." We were finally leaving all of those low-income housing-project–type of apartments and moving into a real house we could finally call home.

The Bible talks about leaving those things that are behind you and looking ahead of you. We were finally leaving that old lifestyle and moving ahead into our first house, in a city called Pomona. We moved onto a street called American Avenue. It felt like we were living the American dream. We were doing really well. We moved into a nice home with a swimming pool. Although the pool was one of those five-foot portable pools, it was a pool, nevertheless. What was fun about the pool was when we would get on the wall and jump down into the pool. My family was so rough on everything. We eventually tore the pool up.

Family Reunion

When we had our family reunions, most of the time they would be held at my mom's cousin's house. On the wall in their living room, they had a beautiful family tree painted in the center of the wall. The tree had our family lineage on it from as far back as my mother's great-great-grandmother. Without exaggeration, I would say there were over one hundred years of history on the wall. It's truly amazing to see this type of history for your family, especially in the black culture, because a lot of our history was destroyed or simply wasn't kept. I truly feel blessed to know somewhat where I came from. There were a lot of names and family members I didn't know anything about. They had young names, as well as old names. In fact, when I got married, my husband's and my name, along with my two daughters' names, were added onto the family tree.

At our family reunions, we had the best barbeque, greens, potato salad, dressing, mac and cheese, homemade hot-water cornbread, and even some things I couldn't even name. We had the best Southern cooks in our family. One of my favorite aunts was the one who made the best hot- water cornbread ever. I would tell my cousin to get me one every time she went into the kitchen. You see, not everyone could go into the kitchen when the adults were in there cooking. My cousin was just old enough to where they wouldn't say anything to her. When I would go over to my aunt's house on a normal day, she would always have the hot-water cornbread on the stove. I still say to this day, nobody made hot-water cornbread like she did.

Chapter 12
Reno, Pink Glass, Not Even Crystal Flamingos

When my mom and stepdad were living in Fresno, my husband and I, along with my mom and my stepdad, went to Reno on a chartered bus. This trip was an overnight trip. We had so much fun. While I was hanging out with my mom, we were playing one particular slot machine. After playing, we left to go and find the guys, and the next thing we knew, they were calling my mom's name on the intercom system, saying her purse had been found. Neither of us had realized she had left it on the slot machine chair where she was playing. Thank God, someone honest found her purse and turned it in to the lost-and-found desk. So, we ran to the lost-and-found desk and got her purse. It wasn't funny at the time, but once we saw everything was accounted for, Mom and I thought it was so funny afterward. We thought to ourselves, who leaves their purse on the back of a slot machine chair and just walks away from it?

Anyway, getting back to the story, it was my stepdad and mom's anniversary. My stepdad showed up an hour later and said he had won a lot of money. He had two pink glass flamingos he had just bought with some of his winnings and gave them to my mom and then said, "Happy anniversary." She said, "Flamingo? Happy anniversary?" with the funniest look on her face. He told her they were expensive. He said he paid a couple of hundred dollars for them.

Later in the day, we just happened to be walking past a gift shop on the Reno mini-strip and we saw the same pink glass (not even crystal) flamingos in the store window. Of course, Mom wanted to go into the store and check the price tag on the flamingos. The price tag showed that the flamingos were only twenty dollars for the pair. This made Mom even madder. That meant each flamingo was only ten dollars apiece. We fell out laughing because we knew my stepdad was lying. He always had the gift to exaggerate about everything. He always made things out to be more than they really were.

My stepdad did have to finally admit he had lied to my mom. While we were all laughing, my mom said she didn't even want the flamingos. She thought he was being cheap. So, the next morning after we ate breakfast, it was time to get on the bus to go home. We all had seats in the front of the bus, which, by the way, was full of passengers. My mom was still mad about getting those damn pink glass (not even crystal) flamingos for her anniversary.

As the bus started on its route home, we started talking about the pink glass (not even crystal) flamingos. Before we realized it, we started arguing on the bus. We hadn't realized the whole bus had gone quiet, and everyone on the bus was now listening to us argue about those pink glass (not even crystal) flamingos.

Once we looked up and noticed the bus had gone completely silent, we noticed everyone was looking at us like, what the hell is going on?

We just started laughing because they were all looking at us, and being the only black family on the bus, we thought they must have wondered whether every black family was like this. After the bus stopped at a predestined rest stop, it felt like everyone was still looking at us. No one said a word as we got back on the bus. Thankfully, the next stop would be home. We laughed about that trip for years.

Vegas, Baby! Here We Come!

A group of us decided to go to Whisky Pete's Casino, located on the Nevada-California state line just inside of Nevada. It was my younger brother's first time being able to gamble and drink legally because he had just turned twenty-one years old. I remember there being a large group of us. My husband, Mom, my sister, one of my older brothers, and I, along with several others, were all hanging out one night in the casino. Once my younger brother found out he could drink all he wanted as long as he was playing, he started telling the waitress, "Keep it coming."

Guess what? She kept it coming. Before you knew it, my younger brother had way too much to drink. So, we decided to go get something to eat, hoping it would help my younger brother sober up. In order to get something to eat, we had to walk through the casino area where the poker tables were located. As we were walking past the poker tables, my brother kept annoying Mom by poking her on the shoulder, to the point where she got so mad at him, she threw her keys at him. Her keys flew halfway across the room, eventually landing under a couple of poker tables.

After we found Mom's keys, we finally made our way over to the restaurant area. As soon as we sat down, my younger brother threw up all over the table. Everybody was looking at us. Thank God, people in Vegas understand how something like this could happen. Nevertheless, it was still embarrassing. Mom was so mad.

We were like, "What? No, he didn't" kind of laughing at the same time. Mom didn't think it was funny. Mom was done with him by then. Mom said, "Get him out of here." My husband and older brother had to literally pick him up and drag him out of the restaurant. He was so drunk, he was laid out as if he were dead. My brother is really tall, so they had to drag him out by his pants. Half of his butt cheeks were hanging out. Once again, how embarrassing, yet funny.

Eventually, they got him to the elevator. They had to lay him up against the wall in order to hold him up, so he wouldn't fall. Once the elevator opened, my husband and older brother had to drag him out of the elevator and to the hotel room. As soon as they got him to the room, they left him there on the floor, to sleep it off.

Chapter 13
The Stolen Car

Early in my relationship when I was dating my boyfriend, now husband, he would always ride his bike over to my house to see me. At this time in his life, he didn't have a driver's license. He was just learning how to drive. So, most of the time when he came by to visit, he would be on his bike. On the other hand, I had my license and was already driving. I would sometimes drive over to his house to see him. So, I thought it was a little strange when he called me one day and said he was coming by to pick me up.

At the time, I didn't think anything of it. I thought maybe his mom had let him drive the car. So, here he came pulling up in my driveway. I came out and got into the car, and we pulled off. We went directly to the freeway and got on. We couldn't have been on the freeway more than five minutes, when a car pulled up right next to us while honking its horn repeatedly. As we started to look over to see what was going on, we were both shocked to see it was his mother and his mother's boyfriend. At this point, I was saying to myself, "What the hell is going on?" Just about the same time, my boyfriend was saying, "Oooooh no."

I was like, "Oh no? What is 'oh no' supposed to mean?" He told me he didn't have permission to be driving the car. "What do you mean, you don't have permission to drive the car?" I asked. He explained he had just taken the car and come by to pick me up. Now mind you, he had already come by to pick me up in the car several times on several different occasions.

"So, you mean to tell me all the other times you came by to pick me up, you didn't have permission? So basically, you've been stealing the car," I angrily responded. Now, as all this was going on in the car, his mother and mother's boyfriend were in the car next to us with looks on their faces that I will never forget.

My boyfriend was so embarrassed and was saying under his breath, "My mom is going to kill me; my mom is going to kill me."

I was telling him, "You should have told me. I wouldn't have gotten into this car with you. I don't want your mother mad at me. She already doesn't like me." Or so I thought.

Now, I know what it's like when people have to read other people's lips. I could clearly see and read His mother's boyfriend's lips. He was pointing at the car and saying, "Pull that damn car over. Pull that damn car over." We eventually got off the freeway and pulled the car over. I thought his mother was going to go off on him right then and there.

My boyfriend started confessing as soon as he got out of the car. He said, "Mommy, I'm sorry. I know I shouldn't have taken the car. I was wrong; I will never do it again." He told her that he just wanted to take me out to get something to eat.

His mother told him to take me home then bring the car home. So, he had to take me home immediately and then drive the car home. The sad thing about it was I never even got to go out to eat dinner with him.

The Night the Television Got Stolen

My older brother played football and was pretty good at it. He played two years at Chaffey College in Rancho Cucamonga, California, and then got a full scholarship to play at San Diego State University (SDSU). After playing for SDSU for two years, he got an opportunity to be drafted by the Saint Louis Cardinals. Upon getting drafted by the Cardinals, there came a huge signing bonus. My mother decided to throw my brother a congratulations celebration party. She invited all of his friends he grew up with. Now mind you, my brother wasn't always the nicest person. As he was growing up in the inner-city, low-income housing projects, he had some friends who were always in trouble, always in and out of jail. So, when Mom decided to throw this celebration party, most of these characters were invited. Even people who weren't invited somehow found their way to the celebration.

We could not believe how many people showed up at this party. There were people everywhere: people in the front yard, people in the den, and people up in the bedrooms. There were people in the backyard. Everyone seemed to be having a great time. Mom was so proud of her oldest son. I can remember seeing that look of pride on Momma's face, not a proud look of being prideful, as to look down on someone, but a look of pride of a great accomplishment. It seemed as if people were saying congratulations every time she turned around.

If memory serves me correctly, I think the party ended around 3:00 a.m. I remember waking up the next morning and seeing some friends still sleeping on the floor. I also remember Mom waking us all up with a loud shout, saying, "Where is my damn television set?" Can you believe it, that after all the partying and good times, someone would actually walk out of the house with Mom's television set? We were all amazed. We were like, "When? How? Why?"

Mom had double doors that led to her bedroom from outside. After thinking about it, this was the only conclusion we could come up with. In the end, when everyone calmed down, we all laughed about it. We thought, the nerves a person would have to have to do something as crazy as this. In the end, it just added to some of the great memories we all had as a family.

Chapter 14
Motherhood

I now had to face the reality of having a baby at the age of seventeen. At the time, they had several programs I was able to apply for. One was Aid to Families with Dependent Children (AFDC), and the other program was called Women, Infants, and Children (WIC). WIC was a special supplemental nutrition program for women, infants, and children. This program was designed to help women who were from low-income families. WIC gave you coupons for milk, eggs, cheese, baby formula, cereal, and a whole host of other things I can't even remember. However, I do remember going to the store and using these WIC coupons. It was so embarrassing. No one wanted to get in your line if you had these coupons because it took forever to process them. My boyfriend would always say, "I'll wait for you in the car." He didn't want to be seen in line while they were processing the coupons.

Once I started to learn how to handle the money the county was giving me, I told my mom it was time for me to get my own place. If you remember, I mentioned earlier that there were always a bunch of people coming over to my mother's house. My brothers' as well as my sister's friends would come over and spend the night.

It didn't matter where they slept. They would just find a spot and fall asleep. I started to become uncomfortable with all of the traffic. This was not how I wanted to raise my child. I started telling Mom at first, then insisting, on being able to move into my own place. Finally, Mom said okay.

I remember calling my boyfriend and telling him I was going to move out. I asked him, "Why don't you move in with me?" At first, he said no, that he wasn't ready to move in and live with me. I mentioned to him, "We already have a baby, so why not?" After several days of talking about it, he finally said, "Yes, let's do it." So, we decided to move in together. Once we moved in together, we started talking about marriage. My boyfriend was totally against getting married. My boyfriend was a basketball player and had a promising career ahead of him. I repeatedly told him getting married would not stop him from doing what he wanted to do.

First, we agreed on engagement and waiting a couple of years. That agreement changed to one year. Finally, we agreed, because we were already living together, that we were going to go ahead and get married in the month of August, one day after his birthday. After we moved in together, less than six months later, we were married. Neither one of us knew what we were getting into. We both claimed to be in love, not knowing we really didn't even know what love was.

So here we were, out on our own, with a now six-month-old baby girl. It's really funny how everyone who met us for the first time thought my boyfriend and I were brother and sister. Everyone thought our daughter was our younger sister because we apparently looked so much alike. Whenever you have a baby, the baby takes on both of the parents' features, so in turn, you start to look like your counterpart.

So, as we began to settle in, my boyfriend got a job working at a convalescence hospital. He would bring home sugar, coffee, spoons, forks, and everything else we needed because we didn't have anything, except for the few things my mother gave me.

Section 8

As I take a look back, I was already married with two children and a husband, all before the age of twenty. This is not the way I had seen my life going, but it was my current situation at the time. I was on a welfare program that gave me cash aid, as well as food stamps to help me feed my family and pay rent. Then I heard about a program called Section 8.

Section 8 was a program where the state assisted you with your rent. For example, if you had to pay six hundred dollars a month for rent, the state would pay about 85 percent of your rent. This came out to roughly 510 dollars that the state would pay. This meant you were responsible for the remaining ninety dollars.

During the time we were on Section 8, my husband decided to go back to school and get his degree in physical education. He always wanted to be a physical education teacher and to coach high school basketball. I, on the other hand, started cleaning houses more regularly, which eventually turned into my cleaning business. I started to see I could make some extra money and at the same time still pick up my kids once the school day ended. We both worked really hard to make it work. We

Taking a Look Back In Order to Move Forward

didn't want to be on Section 8 just because we could pay low rent. We both agreed, however, that we would use it to our advantage. This is where most people make their mistake. They start to get used to paying low rent, and then they settle in and think it's okay, not knowing they're setting themselves up for failure. Most government programs eventually end. We decided that before this program ended on us, I would develop my business, and my husband would get his degree.

During this time, I started putting away money to one day buy a house. This went on for about two years. I can still vividly remember when I told my husband I no longer wanted to be on welfare and Section 8. My husband was having a harder time then I realized. He kept asking me, "Are you sure this is what you want to do?" He tried to convince me to stay on both programs, AFDC and Section 8, a little longer.

Remember, earlier I mentioned I started saving money to move into a house. I would put away every penny I could. We stopped eating out so much. We stopped going out for entertainment. My husband would ask, "Why can't we ever do anything anymore?"

I would just say, "I don't feel like it."

When I believed the day had finally come, and I had saved enough money to make my dream a reality, I told my husband I wanted to start looking for a house to move into. He said, "How are we going to move into a house with no money?" When I told my husband how much money I had saved, he could not believe me. I remember him asking me, "How did you save that much money?"

I said, "Do you recall all the times I said I didn't want to go out and eat or go to the movies? I was saving money."

By this time, I had saved enough for a down payment on a house for a first-time buyer. As I started looking for a house, I came across a great deal on the north side of town. The best part of this was I had saved enough for a house that would be built from the ground up. I got really lucky on this deal. There was no way I was supposed to get a deal like this.

Home Sweet Home

We were so excited about having our home built from the ground up. The best part of this was, we would be the first family to move into the house. It's nice to buy a house; it's even nicer to buy a house that's brand-new and has never been lived in. We were so excited. We would go over to the plot where our brand-new home would be built and try to imagine what was what. We would say things like, "I think this is where the master bedroom will be," or "This is where the three-car garage will be." Those were exciting times. It was about three months before they finally started chalking the ground to lay the foundation for the house.

Once they started laying the foundation for the house, it seemed as if the rest of the house went up fairly quickly. One day we would come by, and they were digging. Another day we would stop by, and the foundation was complete. It seemed a week later that the frame of the house was going up. In no time, the house was built. I can remember when they gave me the keys to move in. Ever since we were married, we had lived in an apartment. We had accumulated so much stuff. When we finally started moving our stuff into the new house, I can remember thinking, "Wow, look at all the space we have."

Forgetting the Past

I had to forgive and forget the past in order to move forward and gain peace with myself. I had to forgive and forget the past in order to move forward for my family and, most of all, for me. God was telling me, "Be still and understand I am God. Be still and understand the purpose I have planned for you." I had to hear what God was telling me to do; I had to mentally fight my way through life. On one occasion, a pastor from Nigeria came to speak at our church, and he called me up to the altar to pray over me. Now normally, I wouldn't go up to the altar. It didn't matter who the pastor was. But for some reason, I was compelled to go to the altar, when he called me to come up. The first thing he told me was I was a fighter. It was profound.

Anyone who knows me knows I am a fighter. So, for this pastor to use this particular phrase, not even knowing who I was and to use those exact words, truly let me know he was a prophetic man of God. At first, I didn't realize what this meant. I always kept so much inside. I didn't know how to release it in a healthy manner. This pastor had the ability to look me in the face and see what I had been going through. When he told me I always had to fight for everything in life, it broke me down.

I thought to myself, finally, there was someone who understood me. As the pastor was praying over me, tears started rolling down my face. I could feel the release of holding things in for years. I finally felt comfortable enough to let it go, and for all practical purposes, I was finally comfortable enough to exhale. If there is anyone who knows me, they know it would have taken a miracle for me to do this in public. I would have never cried in front of people, let alone in front of a church full of people. Now my youngest daughter tells me jokingly, "Mom, you're a fighter. You've had to fight through a lot of things in life. That's what I'm most proud of about you."

Chapter 15
Never Too Much

When my younger daughter was a baby, old enough to sit in her high chair for dinner, sometimes I would give her peas. She would eat everything except her peas. I would say, "You're not getting down until you eat all your peas." I would check on her and she would be leaning over, asleep in the high chair, and those peas would still be on her plate. To this day, she will not eat peas.

When she was a little girl in elementary school, I would tell her, "I will give you ten dollars for every A grade you get." One day she came running home from school to tell me she had gotten straight A's. She wanted her money. We laughed, and I had to pay her for each A grade she received. All in all, she earned around sixty dollars.

When she got ready to go to middle school, she was one of three hundred kids who were picked to go to a school called Compu-tech. Compu-tech was a type of school that prepared students for college at a young age. Compu-tech chose only the brightest students to attend their school. It was an honor for her. She was really excited because she always monitored her grades and wanted to be the best student she could be. She really excelled during middle school. Compu-tech was connected to Edison High School. But because she was chosen to go to Compu-tech, she had classes on both campuses once she got into high school.

After she graduated from high school, she enrolled in Fresno City College. After attending Fresno City College for two years, she received her associate of arts degree (AA) in general education. The following semester she transferred to Fresno State University and majored in medical administration. During this time, she also worked at the church as the administrator for both pastors. While working as the church's administrator, she was lucky enough to travel around the world with her pastors to such places as Ukraine, Israel, Canada, Jamaica, and the Bahamas. She also got the opportunity to travel to other parts of the United States. She traveled to states such as Hawaii, New York, Florida, Georgia, Missouri, Arizona, and Nevada. Even though she went to school and also worked as the church's administrator, she was still able to pursue becoming a certified loan-signing agent.

You would think that would be a heavy-enough load for anyone to carry, but there were other things my daughter accomplished. She passed her bail-bond test to become a bail-bond agent. She passed the test to be a notary public agent. She also became a grant writer. She now works for the Fresno Unified School District as the office manager for a special education school. Now she is writing her first book, called *The Ring: What Every Single Is Looking For*. The book teaches you what to look for in a man or woman in today's world. It teaches you how to spot the warning signs. It teaches you how to wait for a godly husband or a godly wife. That's the wonderful thing about the book: it's for both men and women.

Now, the best part of this story is that, through it all, she still made time in her busy schedule to become an ordained minister of the gospel. The ordination ceremony was awesome. The best part of the ordination was that she and her dad were ordained together. It was one of the most incredible moments in my life—to have a daughter and a husband serving God in such a way that they both got called to a higher level of service. Matthew 22:14 (KJV) tells us, "For many are called, but few are chosen." I'm really proud of the both of them for hearing and accepting their calling.

Chapter 16
The Love of Basketball

God is the only one who knew what my future would be, even before I was born. God knew the guy I dated in high school would eventually become my husband years later. After attending several high schools, I landed at a school called Pomona High School. There was one particular guy who stood out. He had a large Afro and loved playing basketball. Besides basketball, his hair was the second most important thing to him. He would pick his Afro with his fingers instead of using what we called an Afro comb. The reason he picked his hair out with his fingers is that everyone wanted to have a round Afro. So, when he didn't have his comb, he would just pick his hair out with his fingers.

I remember every time he came by my house, he would ask me to braid his hair. He made sure he was always dressed nicely. I used to say to myself, "He has good taste in clothes." Later, I discovered that he was wearing his brother's clothes. I would often hear his brother tell him to stay out of his clothes. His brother would say stuff like, "If you don't stay out of my clothes, I'm going to hurt you."

I would also hear my boyfriend tell his brother, "You're going to have to hurt me because I'm going to wear these clothes." But, in all actuality, his brother didn't mind. He just had to play the big brother role on him.

As our senior year was coming to an end, my boyfriend started getting a lot of awards for his efforts on the basketball court. To name a few, he was a first team All-League player. He was the Most Valuable Player in the league his senior year. He was named first team All-San Gabriel Valley. He was a second team All-Southern California player. He was chosen to represent several all-star teams. He started receiving interest from different universities and colleges to possibly play basketball for them the following year. He received letters of interest from the University of California, University of Washington State, University of Pacific, University of California Fullerton, North Dakota and South Dakota Universities, Pomona Pitzer College, Whittier College, Fresno Pacific College and some I can't even remember.

One of his greatest accomplishments was being nominated to the McDonald High School All-American team. The reason I say it was one of his greatest accomplishments is that only twenty players from each state were chosen. That meant only a total of one thousand players in the entire United States were chosen. Out of one thousand players, only twenty-four players would make what was called the "Dream Team." To even be considered with such accomplished players says a lot about his talent. I'm really proud of him.

Then, some thirty-five years later, he was one of only two players in the history of Pomona High School's existence to have his high school jersey number retired. He wore the number ten. That means no other player will ever get a chance to wear the number ten again. What a fantastic honor.

Reminiscing

When my husband and I were dating, we had a routine of meeting at his locker every day around the same time, which was after third period, because we had a longer break. Also, we would meet in front of the school during lunchtime. I can remember always having money, so every time I went to the snack bar or the store at lunchtime, he would say to bring two of everything, laughing every time he said it. Either he never had money, or he was just trying to see if he could get me to spend mine. Either way, I didn't mind. He had a certain confidence about himself. I just wanted to be with him.

Although we met every day at his locker, as well as in front of the school, we were lucky enough to have an English class together. I remember one assignment we had to do. I was so nervous just sitting next to him, let alone having to speak in front of everyone. I was very shy and didn't like bringing attention my way. Anyway, we had to pick a spelling word and explain to the class what it meant.

I picked the word *passion* because I felt like I was passionately in love with my boyfriend. By now, the whole class knew we were boyfriend and girlfriend. So, what I did was get up and kiss him in front of the entire class—mind you, not even knowing how to kiss. The whole class laughed about it, and even the teacher had to laugh and say that was a good example of passion. I got a B grade for my display of passion.

As time went on, the more we dated, the more we kissed, and the better I got. But, before I learned how to kiss, I would hold my breath.

One day he asked me, "Are you holding your breath?"

I said, "Yes, I thought you hold your breath when you kiss."

He said "No, you don't. You're supposed to breathe out of your nose." So, he showed me how to kiss and breathe out of my nose. He said I had to relax. Since I was always a little nervous around him, that was hard to do at first.

From that point forward, we did everything together. We went everywhere together. One of my favorite dates was the Pomona County Fair. We would take these really big poster pictures. Those were my favorite. We took them every year. The third year we took them, I was pregnant. I was as big as a house. I don't think any of my friends had seen me pregnant before I started showing. It was pretty cool how some of them responded to me. I thought they would be mad at me and would not want to still be my friend. But, on the contrary, they were very happy for me. I thought everyone was going to think I got pregnant on purpose to trap him. After all, he was the most popular guy on campus. He was the best basketball player in the school and possibly the best basketball player in the whole area. I had a girlfriend tell me, she heard rumors in the bathroom, about me being pregnant.

Life-Changing Decision

As school began to come to an end, my boyfriend had to start thinking about where he would go to continue his education, as well as his basketball career. It was one of the hardest decisions he had to make. Remember, he was only eighteen, with a baby on the way. Most young teens would have chosen to go off to college and play basketball. But, for some reason, he decided to stay home and try to go to school locally. He wanted to help raise his daughter. Imagine, being that age and having to make a decision that would change the course of your life forever.

So, my boyfriend decided to go to Cal Poly Pomona University. In reality, he mentioned to me years later, he was only chasing the financial-aid check to help support the family. For example, he went from Cal Poly to Citrus College; then, from Citrus College to Chaffey College, where he did get to play one semester of basketball. At this point in his life, he had finally decided to get serious about school. So, he decided he would finish his two years at Chaffey College and then transfer to Azusa Pacific University to get his bachelor's degree in physical education, now known as kinesiology.

It's amazing how God works in your life. Picture this: Just when he decided to get his life together, a chance of a lifetime would come his way. For three years straight, my boyfriend had been playing in basketball tournaments in Laguna Beach. Some of the best basketball players from California, Nevada, and Arizona would converge at Laguna Beach to play every summer. The tournaments took place every summer, during the first week of each summer month. So, the first weekends of June, July, and August, he, along with his basketball buddies, would travel to Laguna Beach, which was about one and a half hours away from where we lived. These were fun times because we were always on the road traveling everywhere as he played basketball.

One particular summer, while playing at Laguna Beach, he started talking to one of his friends, who happened to be the head basketball coach at Fresno Pacific College. Mind you, for three years, they had always talked after their games. Oftentimes, they would meet up in the championship game, when the tournament got down to the two best teams. So, they already had a personal relationship.

I don't know why the information about him being the head coach of Fresno Pacific College had not come up before. But, for whatever reason, this time it did. I believe my boyfriend was expressing to the coach that he had finally gotten serious about finishing school. He mentioned he wanted to teach physical education and coach high school basketball. He expressed he was going to get his two-year degree and play basketball his second year at Chaffey College.

The coach then said in amazement, "You still have eligibility?"

He told the coach, "I sure do." That's when he formally introduced himself as the head coach of Fresno Pacific College. He offered my husband a scholarship, right there on the beach.

Chapter 17
Fresno, Here We Come

We never thought in our wildest dreams that we would move from the Southern California area, let alone move up north to Fresno. To be honest, we didn't even know where Fresno was. All we knew was it was a great opportunity we couldn't pass up to get his education paid for and to get a college degree out of it. So, the following year, we packed up everything we owned and moved to Fresno to start a new chapter in our lives.

Remember, I said we packed up everything we owned and took a leap of faith that this was the right move for our family. Remember also, I said we didn't even know where Fresno was, truth be told. All we knew was he would be attending a school called Fresno Pacific College and that he would get a chance to finish his education and get his degree. All we knew was he would get the opportunity to play college basketball, the same opportunity he missed out on when he decided to take care of his family and forego his basketball dreams.

What we didn't know was the school he would be attending was an all-white Mennonite Christian school. It was a complete cultural shock. We went from an inner-city type of existence to an all-white existence.

Talk about taking some time to get used to the new environment. On top of that, I didn't even stay with him the first month because the housing situation we were promised was delayed. He ended up staying with some players on campus for the first month.

One month later, the girls and I joined him in our new housing. The best part of having a husband in college, playing basketball, was that our kids got a chance to always be on campus. They would run around, in and out of the gymnasium, throughout his practices. Everyone knew they were our kids, due to the fact there were only three other African Americans on the team. The others were young and did not have any kids.

One of the best things about Fresno Pacific was you could be older and still play. They would call him the old man. If memory serves me correctly, I believe he was twenty-eight years old, while most of the other players were eighteen to twenty years old. Nevertheless, he was excited about getting an opportunity to play basketball and earn his bachelor's degree in physical education.

Hawaiian Sand

During my husband's first year at Fresno Pacific College, the team was scheduled to play in Hawaii. There was another teammate who was also married. The coach decided both wives could go on the trip with the team. So, the coach had the two married couples room together. It was exciting. My husband had never flown on an airplane before, so this would be his first experience. Imagine that. Never flying on an airplane before, and your first opportunity to fly is flying all the way to Hawaii. By the time we got to Hawaii, we had taken off and landed several times, due to the fact we stopped in Las Vegas, Dallas, and then finally to Hawaii. By the time we got to Hawaii, my husband felt like he was an expert in flying and landing.

We got to Hawaii around midnight, and the team had to play early the next morning. The reason this little detail was so important was that during their first game in Hawaii, my husband broke a bone in his foot. Around two hours later, he was in a cast with a walking boot. It really changed all the plans we had for Hawaii. We were there less than one day, with five days to go, making it a total of six days, and he was in a cast with a walking boot.

The next day, the team was given some free time. So, the team all decided to go to the beach. Although we all went to the beach, my husband was not able to get into the water. He was not able to go snorkeling. You know, some people wait a lifetime to go to Hawaii, just to say they snorkeled in the Hawaiian waters. Our friends who did get a chance to snorkel said there were so many different breeds of fish with brilliant colors in the water. They told him it was amazing. I don't know if this helped him or hurt him.

So, we were trying to make the most out of my husband having to wear a cast and a walking boot on his foot. Somehow, the husband of the couple with whom we were rooming and I started playing with the beach sand. I don't quite remember how it happened, but he accidentally threw sand at me, and it got in my face. To be more precise, the sand got all up in my mouth. He thought it was funny and started laughing while slightly running away. His laughing made something rise up in me. I told him, "I'm going to get you for this." Before he knew what happened, I had jumped up and started throwing punches and scratching him. By this time, everyone started to notice the commotion going on down the hill and started running toward us. My husband wasn't too far from us, so he started hopping toward us with the cast and boot on his foot. He got there so fast, you would not have even known he had a cast on his foot. One of their teammates got there first and started pulling me off him. I was furious.

His wife was in shock about what had just happened. Here we were sharing a double room with them, and on the second day of a six-day stay in beautiful Hawaii, this debacle took place. I was on a sandy white beach, fighting her husband, who, by the way, was just about seven feet tall.

The next day, the team had another game. Both couples said very little that night and the next morning. After the game was over, we both apologized to each other. We both admitted it went way too far. We both admitted we should have stopped long before the sand started flying because, by the time I finished, he had so many scratches on him, it looked like Indian war paint. The reason I said it looked like he had Indian war paint on is that they used some natural aloe vera, grown in the Hawaiian Islands, on his scratches. So, he had this reddish, off-green look all over his face and chest. I felt really bad because they were great people.

After everything cooled down, his teammates made fun of him and were saying, "We have a great story to tell, when we get back home." Everyone even made fun of my husband, saying how funny it was seeing him hopping down the hill, like he was going to do something when he got there, with that cast and walking boot on his foot.

Eventually, the trip ended, and we were on our way back to the mainland, once again flying and landing on several different occasions. For someone who had never flown on a plane before, my husband could now be considered an experienced flyer.

Chapter 18
Finally Letting Go

After living in Fresno for three years, the day finally came for my husband to graduate. He would earn his bachelor's degree in physical education. He immediately got into substitute teaching, once he passed his California Basic Education Skill Test (CBEST). I can remember the day he got the letter in the mail. Mind you, he had to take the test three times. He was so confident he would pass the other two sections, he only studied for the math portion of the CBEST. Well, guess what? He only passed the math portion of the test.

When he took the (CBEST) the second time, he only passed the writing section. Finally, on his third attempt, he passed the reading comprehension. He had expressed to me he wasn't sure if he could pass it. He also mentioned to me if he could not pass it, he didn't know what else he could do to fulfill himself. You see, he had always wanted to be a teacher and a coach. So, when he opened the certified letter and noticed it had a passing grade, he literally turned, flipped down the hallway, and yelled, "I passed! I passed!" He knew this was the beginning of his professional career.

Once he passed the CBEST, he started substitute teaching and then got a head coaching position at Fresno High School. He was the girls' basketball varsity head coach. He substituted for nine years before he finally got his single-subject clear teaching credential in physical education, along with a Cross-Cultural Language and Academic Development (CLAD) certificate. Immediately after getting his credential and (CLAD) certificate, he got a full-time teaching position at Rio Vista Middle School, where he taught for one year.

During this time, we purchased a brand-new home. I can remember saying to myself, "Once we buy the house, I know we are never moving back home to Southern California." My husband was now working full time as a physical education teacher and coaching basketball. I was running my own housecleaning business, called Sharp's Cleaning. Although we were settling in, I never wanted to stay in Fresno. The decision to stay in Fresno was one of the biggest causes of our up-and-down relationship at the time. You have to remember, all of our family lived in Southern California.

So, when my mom passed, I was so angry because I had always known, ever since I was a little girl, I would be there when that day came, the day no one ever wants to face, the day when you lose your mother. It was the day when I lost my best friend and support system. I was mad at myself, as well as my husband. For years, he would say we could go back home to visit anytime. Anytime turned out to be mainly holidays, such as Christmas and New Year.

I blamed him at first for not wanting to go home more often so I could see my mother. I was mad at myself for waiting so long between visits. I always felt like we had to go back home as a family until I realized I could've gone back home anytime I wanted. We argued a lot over the years because I had never wanted to move from my hometown in the first place. I did realize, though, it was probably for the best. We could not pass up the opportunity for my husband to get his degree and play college basketball. After all, he did make the sacrifice first by not going away to college right out of high school.

I just wanted to be close to Mom. I should have moved back home when Mom first got sick. The guilt I was feeling was so bad. I carried that guilt for the longest time, blaming myself. I also hated my sister because she never told me how sick our mom really was. She never told me Mom had cancer. All she told me was I had better take the next train smoking home. I wish she would have just called me like a big sister should have and told me what was going on with our mom. She had always wanted to see me fall apart. She knew this would literally tear me apart.

She always said to me, "You're not here," and I hated her so much. She made it about her and what she was doing for our mother, not about us as a family. By then, my mom had gotten very sick. It pains me to say this, but she was dying. I asked my stepdad if he could bring her to me. By then, she was too weak to travel. Besides, she didn't want me to worry about her or what she was going through. Mom never wanted to be a burden to her five kids; this is why she never told us how serious her condition was.

It took everything in me, for years, to finally realize Fresno was okay. But there was a time in the beginning, when I told my husband, "I'm leaving and going back home, and I'm taking the kids with me." I was missing home and my mom. Ultimately, though, I think God was telling me to be still. I think this was one of the first times I can honestly say I heard God speak to me clearly. So, I stayed because we were just starting to build a family and a name for ourselves.

I think all the time about what I could have done differently. If I had a chance to change anything, it would be to tell Mom every day how much I loved and needed her and how much her advice meant to me. I would have told her how her wisdom kept me out of trouble. I would have told her that her sincerity allowed me to grow up with great character and integrity. I would have let her know the way she loved me unconditionally allowed me to be confident in the way I now loved my husband and children, which was also unconditionally.

I never really understood my sister when we were growing up. We always shared a room together and slept in the same bed. She didn't know it, but I really looked up to her. However, when I became a teenager, got pregnant, and had a baby, things seemed to change all at once. This is when a lot more of the competition, jealousy, and mean-spiritedness started to show what type of person she really was.

My sister seemed like she never wanted me to get more attention than she did. She became my worst enemy. For years, we had a love-hate relationship. But the one thing my sister finally admitted to me was she was jealous of the relationship Mom and I developed over the years. We did everything together. We would go have lunch and then get our nails done. Or, we would cook food together and sit at home and watch our favorite television shows. That would be enough for the both of us. But my sister was jealous of the relationship Mom and I had.

Even when my sister went through the worst of times, I was there for her the way family should be there for each other during times of distress and chaotic situations. As we were growing up together in the same household, she was the kind of person you just didn't want to be around. I thought when our mom passed away, she would change her ways, but she didn't. I didn't like a lot of things about my sister, but in my heart, I have always loved her. I thought maybe by now, I could move on and heal from all the hurts and pains my sister has caused me. It's been really hard. To be honest, I don't know if I will ever be able to put all the hurts and pains behind me. But I'm going to try.

Chapter 19
Taking a Look Back in Order to Move Forward

By writing this book, I wanted to use it as a way of closing the door on the past and begin moving forward. There were two major events in my life that were the catalysts to my writing this book. One was when my mother died. The second was when I found out there were never any papers filed for my marriage license. Those two events started me down memory lane. This is when I started taking a look back in order to try to move forward. Sometimes we feel as though our lives are insignificant. We feel as though we haven't accomplished anything, that we have nothing to offer. We say things like, "If I had it to do all over again, I would do things differently," when in fact, if we would just take a moment to look back, we would see we did a lot more then we give ourselves credit for.

This book was also used as a way to heal from all of life's traumatic experiences. You can't imagine how I must have felt when I found out that a marriage license had never been filed. By law, for all practical purposes, I was never married. I felt incomplete. I felt like my

Taking a Look Back In Order to Move Forward

life was a big lie. The first thing I wanted to do was to renew my wedding vows and have a wedding ceremony.

By writing this book, it has allowed me to go through grief, as well as healing, after the passing of my mother. The day I found out Mom had passed away was devastating for me. It felt like my world was over. I was full of guilt, grief, and depression because I wasn't there when she went on to be with the Lord. The pain I felt was excruciating. It was a pain I had never experienced before. How do you reconcile the death of a parent? I went into a complete tailspin. I would wake up from my sleep with anxiety attacks.

The thing I missed the most was the daily conversations Mom and I would have. Even when we didn't agree, we would not let a day go by without talking to each other, even if it was to just say, "I'm still mad at you" for whatever we were mad about. Most of the time, we couldn't even figure out what we were mad about. All I know is if I didn't know God, I would not have made it. By writing this book, it has allowed me to put things in proper perspective. I know Mom would be proud of me. The one takeaway I have is that Mom would want me to go on in life and do great things. Well, Mom, I pray by writing this book, it has made you proud of me. I will always love you.

By writing this book, it has also taken me back down memory lane. I was able to reminisce about my childhood, like the time I was in a serious car accident that left me in the hospital for six months and a full body cast for six weeks after that. I thought about the time our family lived in these low-income housing projects, when all we could afford was government-issued commodity food, and we got most, if not all, of

Taking A Look Back In Order To Move Forward

our Christmas gifts from a truck that used to come by and give away free toys. It brought me back to the times when we would have those crazy family fights. Sometimes I look back and ask myself, how did we ever make it? We didn't have anything. But, the one thing we did have was a house full of love.

By writing this book, it has allowed me to look back on some of my fondest high school memories, like the first time I laid eyes on my soul mate—this handsome young man who loved basketball and his Afro. Through his passion for basketball, it brought our family to Fresno and a new life adventure. We were now known as the "sharp" family. It was different because everyone knew us from high school. We had a good reputation in our hometown. Now we would have to start over. As the years passed, I remember getting the opportunity to purchase my first home. As I look back, I can remember how excited I was. We were having a house built from the ground up. We were the first family to ever live in the house. It's now been sixteen years. Wow, how time flies.

When I look back, I see how much love we shared as a family, as my daughters wrote beautiful letters of encouragement when I was down. Also, my daughter wrote a heartfelt Father's Day timeline card, detailing some of her memories about the family.

When I take a look back, I can't help but think about the time my husband got me a dog for Christmas. I never, ever, wanted a dog. I was furious. Now, I can't live without the dog. I don't know what I would do without Diamond. Yes, the dog's name is Diamond. Imagine going from not wanting a dog to developing a product that would take me to *Shark Tank* for an opportunity to pitch a product I developed called Sharp's Doggie Padded Panties, a product for dogs who are in heat. I even came up with a brilliant slogan, which said, "Beat the Heat, and Keep It Neat."

Through it all, the good and the bad, by writing this book, it has allowed me to look at life from a new perspective. I no longer think about all the things I thought I missed out on, but now I look at all the things I got to do. My prayer for you is, by reading this book, you will gain a greater perspective about your life. May you see your life as being full and complete. May you see your life as a glass of water that is half-full and not half-empty. Remember, it's the same glass of water. It's just how you see it. Amen.

About the Author

Tina Sharp was born in Riverside, California, and grew up in Ontario, California. She presently lives in Fresno, California. Tina was married at the tender age of seventeen to Johnny Sharp, her high school sweetheart, and they have been married for thirty-eight years. Tina is a wife and a mother of two daughters, Renishia and Tenishia Sharp. Tina is now a retired entrepreneur, having created serval businesses. Sharp's Cleaning Service was her main business, which she ran for twenty-five years before retiring. She was proud of her slogan because it represented who she was in business: "You tried the rest; now try the best."

Tina was also a Walmart vendor for a product called Sharp's Doggie Padded Panties. The product was for dogs in heat. Her slogan was "Beat the heat, and keep it neat." Tina also developed her own barbeque sauce that was sold locally. During Thanksgiving and Christmas, she always sold dream pies and sweet potato pies. Now her goal is to become one of the top authors on the West Coast.

CPSIA information can be obtained
at www.ICGtesting.com
Printed in the USA
FSHW020635211219
64958FS